TAROT FOR BEGINNERS

A Guide to Psychic Tarot Reading, Real Tarot Card Meanings, and Simple Tarot Spreads

BY LISA CHAMBERLAIN

Tarot for Beginners

Published by **Wicca Shorts**

ISBN: 1507775555

ISBN-13: 978-1507775554

Disclaimer

No part of this publication may be reproduced or transmitted in any form or by any means, mechanical or electronic, including photocopying or recording, or by any information storage and retrieval system, or transmitted by email without permission in writing from the publisher.

While all attempts have been made to verify the information provided in this publication, neither the author nor the publisher assumes any responsibility for errors, omissions, or contrary interpretations of the subject matter herein.

This book is for entertainment purposes only. The views expressed are those of the author alone, and should not be taken as expert instruction or commands. The reader is responsible for his or her own actions.

Adherence to all applicable laws and regulations, including international, federal, state, and local governing professional licensing, business practices, advertising, and all other aspects of doing business in the US, Canada, or any other jurisdiction is the sole responsibility of the purchaser or reader.

Neither the author nor the publisher assumes any responsibility or liability whatsoever on the behalf of the purchaser or reader of these materials.

Any perceived slight of any individual or organization is purely unintentional.

YOUR FREE GIFT

As a way of showing my appreciation for purchasing my book, I'm offering a free downloadable book, exclusive to my readers.

Wicca: Book of Wiccan Spells is ideal for any Wiccans looking to start practicing Witchcraft. It includes a collection of ten spells that I have deemed suitable for beginners.

You can download it by visiting:

www.wiccaliving.com/bonus

I hope you enjoy it!

CONTENTS

INTRODUCTION

The Tarot has long been a subject of curiosity.

Since their first rise to popularity in the European Renaissance, Tarot cards have captivated the imaginations of people all over the globe. While they began as playing cards, these decks evolved into a method of divination still widely used today. If you've ever wanted a Tarot reading, or wondered what it takes to become a Tarot reader, this guide provides an informative first look into this long-trusted tradition.

"Divination" is the act of seeking knowledge of the unknown, particularly knowledge of the future, by "supernatural" means. Divination has been practiced, in one form or another, all over the world since ancient times. It's an umbrella term that encompasses a variety of occult processes, such as palm reading, scrying, or consulting the I-Ching.

Some practitioners of divinatory arts consider the information they gain as being inspired by a higher power, while others attribute it to intuition. Some consider both to be part of the process. The different forms of divination are all used for the same purpose; to read signs, omens, or events in order to offer some form of advice to a *querent*—another word for the person with a question. (If you're reading the cards for yourself, *you* are the querent.)

There is a myth that you need to have "psychic powers" to read Tarot cards, but all you really need is determination and the willingness to focus on honing your natural intuition. Reading the Tarot is a combination of skills born from following instructions, listening to intuition, and making educated leaps of thought. As complicated as it may seem at first, it's actually a relatively simple process. Seasoned Tarot readers would say that it's a natural habit—something that comes like second nature to them. You too can reach that level of experience and comfort with the Tarot, through practice and patience.

If you're looking for guidance in the way you live your life, the Tarot could be just what you're looking for. Those who read Tarot have a tendency to read the cards for themselves and use them to help when it comes to making difficult decisions. Sometimes, the cards lead their reader to ideas that they wouldn't have come up with on their own.

Tarot is also a great way to deepen the connection with yourself and your intuition. The Tarot can help you understand yourself in ways that you hadn't thought to investigate before. They'll also teach you stronger ways to tap into the resources that you have locked away inside of yourself.

This guide provides the resources needed to introduce beginners to the art of Tarot. You'll find a brief overview of the history of the cards and the components of a standard deck, as well as an introduction to the general meanings of each card, the basics of two common layouts, and guidelines for approaching the reading process. You'll also find tips for choosing your own deck and creating ideal conditions for powerful readings.

However, because the Tarot is a different experience every time, for every practitioner, know that you'll be personalizing the information presented here as you move forward in your path to becoming a seasoned reader. Use your intuition as you go, being sure to keep what makes sense, disregard what doesn't, and stay open to ideas that come "flashing" to your mind as you read. Remember, in any divination method, your intuition is key.

There's no time to start practicing with it like the present, so let's dive straight in!

A BRIEF GUIDE TO TAROT HISTORY

While the history of the Tarot is at least a few centuries old, the use of the cards specifically for divination purposes came about more recently. And although various myths persist about the origins of Tarot cards, there is no single creator of an "original" deck, and no true original order for the cards in the Major Arcana. Rather, the Tarot evolved over time and through the contributions of many people.

The first cards known to historians that resemble the modern Major Arcana appeared in the early 1400s in Italy, although they were found in other places in Europe fairly shortly after that. The nobles of medieval society played games with a deck of cards that were somewhat like modern playing cards, in that they had four numbered suits, each of which had its own symbol. The new "trump" cards were added as a fifth suit, and used to play a game that became the ancestor of modern bridge. These early Major Arcana were not quite like the decks we use now. They were not named or numbered, and there may have been a fairly wide variety of characters, depending on the time period and the region they were created in.

It was in France that the cards became the source of occult interest—an interest that continues to this day. In the region of

Marseilles, the trump cards began to be standardized, in that they became consistently numbered with Roman numerals, in a largely consistent order, and were given titles. By the end of the 16th century, this standardization was more or less complete. Many different manufacturers created the decks, but they were all very similar. This synthesis became known as the Tarot of Marseilles, and the version of it most familiar to modern readers was first published in 1748.

A few decades later, occult interest in the Tarot started to bloom, and claims were made that the decks were based on ancient Egyptian knowledge that came down through the centuries. Later occultists began to develop theories that related the Tarot to the letters of the Hebrew alphabet and the mystical Kabbalah, as well as astrological signs and the elements.

It was during this time that the terms "Major Arcana" and "Minor Arcana" came into use. (The word "arcana" comes from the Latin word for "secret" or "mystery.") The newer versions of Tarot decks were designed around divination purposes explicitly, drawing from these newer mystical associations. Even after the idea of an Egyptian origin was dismissed, the other associations remained, and continue to influence and inform many Tarot readers to this day.

Eventually, the Tarot came to interest British occultists of the 19th and early 20th centuries, who were influenced by the ideas of the French. In particular, the cards interested members of the Hermetic Order of the Golden Dawn, an organization that heavily influenced modern occultism in many ways.

It was through this group that poet Arthur Edward Waite and artist Pamela Colman Smith came to create the most popular—and arguably the most influential—Tarot deck of the 20th century. It was based on the Tarot of Marseilles, but with an important difference—it provided illustrations for the pip (numbered) cards, rather than simply using the corresponding number of symbols to represent the suit. (One other known deck, from late-15th century Italy, had illustrated pip cards, and Smith drew some of her inspiration from an exhibit of the cards at the time of creating the new deck.)

This was the first full Tarot deck designed exclusively for divination, and is widely credited with popularizing the Tarot, which had once been more or less exclusively studied in secret by occult societies. It has been known as the Rider-Waite deck, crediting the original publishers, William Rider & Son, but has more recently, and accurately, been called the Waite-Smith deck, in order to give due credit to the artist responsible for the images on the cards.

Interest in the Tarot grew quietly over the next few decades, until it reached unprecedented popularity in the U.S. in the 1960s. Since that time, a variety of new decks, philosophies, and approaches to reading the Tarot have developed. Where occultists used to argue for a specific set of interpretations that must be memorized in order to read the cards, 21st-century mystics see these things differently, emphasizing intuition over rigorous study. Many argue that as society develops and changes, so do the messages available in the Tarot. However, it is still considered useful to begin "at the beginning," with a basic understanding of the principles of Tarot as they were developed through the Tarot of Marseilles, and later, the Waite-Smith deck.

SECTION ONE

THE MODERN TAROT DECK

THE TAROT DECK

The Tarot deck as we now know it contains a total of 78 cards, divided into the Major and Minor Arcana. Each section has its purpose in reflecting inner truths and hidden knowledge.

Using the deck as a whole, the interaction of the Major and Minor cards can provide a complex picture of various unseen forces at play in a given situation. The Minor cards can help contextualize the spiritual lessons of the Major cards, and the archetypes behind the Major cards can point to what we're meant to be learning from seemingly ordinary circumstances.

Let's take a closer look at each element of the Tarot deck.

THE MAJOR ARCANA

The heart of the Tarot is the Major Arcana.

These cards, which are often referred to as the "trump cards," are the most powerful in the deck. They deal with major issues in life, rather than the more mundane ups and downs of everyday existence.

Each card depicts a character, or archetype, which represents a stage on our spiritual journey from complete innocence to hard-earned wisdom. There are 22 trump cards in all, often numbered in Roman numerals from I to XXI (1 to 21), with the first card, The Fool, given a "0."

The sequence of cards in the Major Arcana has been referred to as "the Fool's journey." The Fool is the first card in the group (in most decks), and represents the "blank slate" with which we all enter life, as well as the ignorance we maintain if we fail to learn anything from our experiences. Laid out in order from 0 to 21, the cards tell the story of what happens once the Fool steps forward into the journey of spiritual development.

The final card in the sequence is the World, signifying the fulfillment that comes with having learned and integrated the lessons the Fool encounters along his journey. In between these two are the other twenty trump cards. Some, like the Fool, depict archetypal characters, such as the Empress, the Devil, and the Hermit, while others represent celestial bodies—the Sun, the Moon, the Star—or certain qualities of character, such as Temperance and Strength.

The sources for the names of the trump cards are not entirely known, but are thought to have come from religious, historical, and mystical influences in medieval and earlier European cultures.

It should be noted that in some decks, the Fool card is not numbered at all, while in others, he is the final card in the Major Arcana, rather than the first. These differences may seem quite contradictory, but it makes sense when you consider that the Fool's Journey is cyclical rather than linear. Once we've learned a particular life lesson, we're ready to pursue a new one, which often means starting back at the beginning.

In any Tarot spread, it is especially important to pay attention to any Major Arcana cards making an appearance. If you have several trump cards in a reading, then it's likely that you are, or will be, experiencing some events which will heavily influence your life in the long term. In order to delve further into your spiritual and personal quest, it is vital that you pay attention to the important lessons the cards are presenting to you.

Major Arcana cards outweigh all other cards in a spread, so if there are two interpretations at odds with each other, the interpretation of the Major Arcana card "trumps" the other. They also raise the significance of the position they fall in, so that, for example, a trump card in your Past position means that aspect of your past is an important influence on your current situation. Any reversed Major Arcana cards may be indicating that you're oblivious, or at least not paying enough attention, to the relevant life lesson, and will find it hard to progress in your life until you address the concerns being indicated by the reversed card.

The Major Arcana cards can be seen as pointing the way to spiritual self-awareness; as such they hold deep and meaningful lessons.

THE MINOR ARCANA

The Minor Arcana, sometimes called the Lesser Arcana, makes up the bulk of the deck.

There are fifty-six Minor Arcana cards in a standard deck, divided into four different suits of fourteen cards each: Wands, Cups, Swords, and Pentacles. Each of the suits contains ten numbered cards, which are sometimes referred to as the "pip" cards.

As in traditional playing cards, the first card of each suit is represented as an Ace, rather than the number one. The numbered cards are followed by four Court cards, usually called the Page, the Knight, the Queen, and the King. Some decks vary these titles, using Knaves for Pages, for example. The names for the suits can vary more widely, particularly in the French decks. Some of these alternate names are provided in the introduction to each suit, below.

The cards in the Minor Arcana are believed to represent the more concrete or mundane elements of everyday life, as opposed to larger aspects of spiritual development or major, life-altering events. Each suit is centered on a particular realm of experience: ideas, feelings, action, or manifestation, details of which will be explained below. It is said that these cards describe the situation that the querent is experiencing. However, within this second group of cards are two subgroups that are seen as having special or significant meanings: the Aces, and the Court Arcana.

As the first cards of each suit, the Aces represent the qualities of their suits in their purest form.

They signal beginnings, and are often considered to hold the "seed" or absolute potential of a situation. As with any card, *where* they appear in a reading will determine *how* they are interpreted. For example, if the Ace of Wands appears in a reading in the "near future" position, it could signal that you will soon be coming upon an inspiring idea that will help you see a solution to a particular problem. If this card were in the "past" position instead, it would be assumed that this idea has already appeared. Aces are considered to be special cards with more power than the regular numbered cards, as they represent the unlimited potential of the forces that shape our lives.

The Court Arcana is the collective term for the Pages, Knights, Queens and Kings of each suit. These cards are generally thought to represent individual people and their influence on a situation, though they may reflect a personality trait within the querent that is either helping or hindering progress. Pages are often seen as messengers bringing some kind of news, while Knights, associated with swift-moving energy, often herald a sudden change in a situation. Queens and Kings represent the feminine and masculine ruling influences of their given suits. For example, the Queen of Cups represents the ideals of using emotional intelligence for the benefit of all, while the King of Swords may indicate an authoritative, competent problem-solver.

As you begin to get a feel for how Tarot works, you may want to pay attention to any Aces or Court cards that show up in your readings—particularly if they seem to show up with any frequency!

OCCULT CORRESPONDENCES

As mentioned previously, the evolution of the Tarot as a means of divination arose at least in part from a belief that the cards had strictly mystical origins.

Regardless of what is now known about the history of the Tarot, many of these mystical associations have remained, and are considered by many contemporary readers to offer useful insight into the cards. Some Tarot traditions are still rooted in the association between the Major Arcana and the Kabbalah, and there are particular spreads and even decks that center on this connection. Astrological correspondences are also commonly acknowledged, with each card linked to a sign of the Zodiac, a celestial body, or both. The four classical elements are acknowledged in most traditions, too, with each suit having the characteristics of either Earth, Air, Fire, or Water. These correspondence systems can vary widely, depending on the source, but nonetheless have the potential to add interest and insight to the Tarot experience.

Perhaps the most widely recognized esoteric "crossover" is the recognition of numerological messages among the cards, likely because the cards are numbered in every Tarot deck.

Numerology tends to focus mostly on the numbers 1-9, so each of the pip cards is automatically assigned, while the higher-numbered cards in the Major Arcana are reduced through addition to their single-digit equivalent. (For example, Temperance, which is number 14, would be considered a 5, from adding 1 and 4.) The same can be done for the Court cards, although many traditions consider the Courts to be unnumbered. Paying attention to the numbers on the cards can add an extra layer of meaning to a reading, particularly if several cards with the same number appear.

Of course, familiarity with the esoteric meanings of the numbers themselves is necessary to make the most out of this angle of card reading, which is rather a lot to take on when you're just starting out with Tarot. Nonetheless, if you find that a certain number or pair of numbers keeps showing up in your readings, it's probably worth looking up the mystical associations in a numerology source, as numbers are a popular way for the Universe to communicate with us!

SECTION TWO

TAROT CARD MEANINGS

REVERSED CARDS

In the next section, you'll find general meanings for each of the cards in the Tarot.

The main meaning is first, followed by the "reversed" meaning, which applies when the card appears upside down from the *querent's* perspective. Reversed meanings are quite often the opposite of the upright meaning, although this isn't always the case—sometimes, particularly with cards that have a negative indication when they're upright, the reversed meaning is simply a more intense version.

There is some debate over whether reversed meanings are appropriate or necessary, and not all Tarot readers use them.

Some readers will periodically sort through their decks to be sure that each card is facing the same way so that reversed cards never appear. On the other hand, others actually ensure that reversed cards *will* appear, by turning sections of the deck around when cutting it before the reading begins. These readers find that reversed cards add an extra depth to the reading that can't be discovered if all the cards are facing the same way. Some will argue that the reading is too "one-sided" if the reverse meanings are ignore, but others will say that focusing more on the interaction or "conversation" among all the cards in the spread is really what provides the most accuracy.

One reason for the varying approaches regarding reversed cards is likely the fear of "bad news." In fact, many people who shy away from the Tarot and/or other divination systems do so for fear of finding out that some horrible thing awaits them in the future. This fear is misplaced, however, because the future is never set in stone. A quality Tarot reading will provide you with a view of what is likely to happen in the future if you stay on your current course. It will also provide you with advice on how to change that scenario, if you wish to do so. However, if you are inclined to believe negative or unfavorable predictions, you have a pretty good chance of seeing them realized, since our true beliefs shape our reality!

It's also important to realize that a reversed card in any position does not automatically mean "bad news." Often, it may simply indicate a "lack of good news" or a delay in events you're anticipating. Depending on the deck and interpretation style of any given reader, a reversed card may simply show a different angle on the theme represented by the card as a whole.

Whether to use reversed meanings is entirely up to you.

When you're just starting out, there's plenty to learn just from using the upright meanings, so you might consider waiting until you're more experienced before deliberately involving reversed meanings. (However, if you are intentionally keeping all the cards upright and one still ends up reversed, which has been known to happen, then you may want to consider that a particular message to keep in mind!)

AN INTRODUCTION TO THE CARDS

Now we'll take a brief look at each card individually, in terms of what they represent and how they might be interpreted within a reading.

While these descriptions are accurate in a general sense, it's important to realize that each deck has its own subtle individualities that may lead to differences from the interpretations you find here. For example, the imagery on any given card must be paid close attention, as it will offer you more nuanced meanings and messages than the title of the card alone can provide. This guide only focuses on the title of the card, however, in order to be useful to those with decks that may or may not resemble the imagery on the Waite-Smith or Marseilles decks.

Keep in mind that these are general meanings. In a reading, they will likely be altered at least to some extent by their position in the spread and their relationship to the other cards. But the information below provides a baseline from which to get more familiar with the cards of the Tarot.

THE CARDS OF THE
MAJOR ARCANA

0
THE FOOL

The Starting Point.

The Fool is just about to set off on the journey. This is the zero point from which everything transpires.

Because nothing is yet known here at the origin of the Fool's journey, both optimism and caution are called for. Beginning a new journey is a time to feel hopeful, courageous, and even young at heart. However, there may be risks ahead as well.

Who will you encounter? What will you learn? How will the choice you make next ultimately come to affect your circumstances? Sometimes, this is impossible to know. Letting go of *thinking* you know, or that you *need* to know, is a good place to start. With this card, the only thing you can control is taking the first step.

If The Fool is laid upright, it can signify innocence, a free spirit, spontaneity and beginnings.

However, if the card is reversed, it can point to recklessness, risk-taking, general foolishness, and naivety. Proceed with open-minded caution.

I
THE MAGICIAN

In the sequence of Major Arcana Tarot cards, The Magician is the number one, which represents beginnings.

The Fool encounters the Magician first among the trump characters because, having taken the step forward that begins the journey, he has set magical forces in motion.

This card signifies initiations and acting on one's will. It is associated with energy, creativity, new projects, and a call to adventure. It is also a reminder that the Universe mirrors each of our actions in the greater scheme of things, so we should take care to direct our energy wisely. The Magician is associated with the planet Mercury, which points to the use of skill, logic, and intellect when taking action. The Magician bridges the spirit world and the human world together, making possible the manifestation of our goals.

If the card is laid upright, The Magician can represent skill, concentration, power, action, and resourcefulness. Positive conditions for success in a new endeavor can be taken advantage of.

However, if the card is reversed, it could represent manipulation, poor planning, or even trickery. There may be others in the situation who don't have your best interests at heart. Or, you may simply be suffering from a creative block.

II
THE HIGH PRIESTESS

The High Priestess signifies wisdom, femininity, intuition, the past, secrets, and spirituality.

As the second character of the Major Arcana, she is the mediator of imagination and assimilation, and her association with the Moon suggests mystery and intuition. This card often appears when changes are taking place on the inner planes that will be released into outer reality at the appropriate time. Although we may be at the early stages of a spiritual journey, none of us is really a truly blank slate—we bring memories of the past and emotional associations to every act and every experience. This card acknowledges the inner forces at work in our responses to external circumstances.

When The High Priestess is upright, the card can represent mystery, the subconscious and even higher powers of the mind. Your intuition is growing stronger and you're encouraged to trust your instincts. You may be keeping emotions and/or secrets closely hidden at the present moment, until you know it is safe to reveal them.

Reversed, this card can point to hidden agendas on the part of others, or even hidden from yourself in your own subconscious. Either way, be careful about whom you entrust with emotional truths at this time.

III
THE EMPRESS

The Empress card is ruled by Venus, the planet of love, fertility, harmony, art, creativity, grace, and beauty.

As the number 3 character in the deck, she represents the creative expression of the inspiration and intuition of the first two cards. At this stage in the spiritual journey, we learn that we create the world and reality we live in through our thoughts, words, and deeds. How do we want to shape our circumstances?

When shown upright, The Empress can stand for beauty, abundance, fertility, and femininity. This card may relate to marriage and pregnancy, or the positive influence of a mother figure. She is a good omen for stable, committed relationships. Harmony in the home is also indicated here.

However, reversed, the card can signify a block to independent creativity, or an over-reliance on others. There may be difficulties with an older woman, possibly a mother, aunt, or grandmother. Watch out for clinginess, jealousy, and/or an unhealthy response to money issues, either in yourself or in others.

IV
THE EMPOROR

The Emperor is the male compliment to The Empress, and signifies fatherhood, action, relationships, authority, and guidance.

As the number 4 character, the Emperor is associated with construction, formation and solidity. This is where we learn that we rule ourselves and our domain, the physical manifestation of the creative expression in the previous card. We also learn that there is great power in structure and self-control.

The Emperor may appear in a reading to announce the appearance of someone or something that will change the status quo, possibly presenting an opportunity to enter into a new partnership or lifestyle.

Upright, the card suggests that protection, advice, and/or support are coming from a trustworthy male figure. He may be authoritarian or seem old-fashioned, but he has strength of purpose and is worth listening to, especially when it comes to issues of building lasting support structures.

However, The Emperor reversed can warn of domination, inflexibility, excessive control and even rigidity. You or someone you know is losing perspective on the situation: take a step back and remember that flexibility is the necessary counterpart to solid structure.

V
THE HIEROPHANT

Hierophant means "high priest" in Greek, and this card is somewhat of a masculine compliment to The High Priestess.

Representing wisdom, practical knowledge, guidance, progress, and divinity, this card reminds us that our journey is best guided by belief and tradition as we search for truth and understanding.

As the 5th character in the Major Arcana, this card carries the energies of change and expansion, which are best balanced with tradition and conformity. If the High Priestess points to the inner mystery of our experience, the Hierophant points to its outward expression, where we have to determine the difference between right and wrong.

Upright, the religious figure of The Hierophant can signify the benefits of identifying with tradition and practical wisdom. It can also indicate that you are about to embark on a new opportunity that will bring you closer to your soul's purpose. Now is a good time to take advice from someone you trust, perhaps a mentor who can help you resolve a challenge.

Reversed, however, this card may actually be advising you to challenge the status quo, at least in your personal belief system. Beware of the influence of an oppressive, older person who wants you to do things their way regardless of your actual circumstances.

VI
THE LOVERS

The Lovers card points to decisions, love, growth, and maturity.

As the 6th card in the Major Arcana, it carries the energy of adjustment, and points to how our experience of this life is affected by our relationships with others. While The Lovers can point to romantic love and sexuality, it is more often associated with the challenges of making choices that involve or affect others, or dealing with choices others make that affect us. Bound up in this fact of life is the question of our individual values and whether they align with our current circumstances. As such, the situation indicated by this card might involve sudden and unpredictable changes, or the more gradually dawning understanding that one has outgrown a relationship or an environment.

Upright, The Lovers card can predict some element of love, choices, unions, relationships, or positive alignment between one's beliefs and actions. It may be that a successful decision is to be made, grounded in careful self-examination and foresight. Previous tensions or conflict will be resolved. You are being advised to follow your heart and intuition if you are to take a leap toward achieving a goal.

The Lovers card read reversed could indicate a misalignment of values, or disharmony in an area of life related to relationship with others or with self. Commitment issues and/or break-ups may be indicated, especially if one partner would rather pull away than work through difficulties. Whatever comes of the choice made by you or someone you care about, it will ultimately be for the good.

VII
THE CHARIOT

The Chariot card speaks to the element of our spiritual journey that involves determination, forward movement, willpower, and self-control.

While literal travel may be indicated in some readings, the metaphorical meaning has more to do with setting out on the road to self-mastery. We are no longer stepping blindly into new adventure, but setting a more determined course, having prepared for victories by learning the lessons we've encountered so far along the Fool's journey.

Preparedness is key to success, however. In the Greek tragedy of Phaeton and the Chariot, young Phaeton's impetuous, over-confident nature causes him to lose control of the chariot that pulls the Sun across the sky, ending in Phaeton's death and disaster for the Earth. This card reminds us to respect the power of our own will and use it wisely.

The Chariot upright signifies determination, assertion, and a drive for adventure. You have the ability to use your own will to gather the forces together which will move you toward a new relationship or career situation.

When the card is reversed, it indicates a lack of control and direction, as well as the pitfalls of aggression, ego, and arrogance. It may also be that progress has come or will soon come to a halt, or that you feel you're going in wrong direction.

VIII
STRENGTH

The Strength card acknowledges that we struggle, as imperfect beings, with desires and instincts that may not always be best to pursue.

This card's astrological sign is Leo, the sign of the Lion who is associated with strength and potentially dangerous ferocity. This card points to the qualities of patience, courage, and confidence in the face of risk, and indicates that powerful spiritual forces may be at work in your life at this time.

Upright, Strength points to compassion, endurance, patience and courage. Persistence is needed to face a potentially dangerous opponent. Aims can be achieved with quiet confidence rather than displays of overt strength. You are being encouraged to exert control over your life through love rather than force.

Reversed, this card may be revealing self-doubt, a lack of self-discipline, or some other weakness. You may be avoiding dealing with difficult emotions like anger and are therefore prevented from moving past an obstacle. The inclination to run away rather than risk confrontations will ultimately cause more harm than it's worth. Alternatively, you may be being advised to curb baser instincts, such as overindulgence in food or drink.

IX
THE HERMIT

The Hermit is a pioneer of discovery who lights the way for others. Associated with inner knowledge, withdrawal, isolation and self-discovery, this card reminds us that as we search for our own intellectual and spiritual wisdom, we have to spend some time in seclusion.

Less literally, the card can also signify the need to go against the grain of the conventional wisdom we've inherited from our families and societies, even if we remain physically in their presence. Whatever the case, an important component of this card is the eventual sharing of knowledge, since there's not much point in keeping one's spiritual discoveries entirely to one's self. The Hermit is committed to going forward on his path toward the ultimate goal of sharing all awareness.

Upright, the Hermit may signify a state of solitude and searching, whether in academic study or soul-searching. This card predicts you'll be rewarded for your solitary work, not in the least through stronger inner guidance than you've had before. The Hermit can also signify the need for recuperation after an illness or a harrowing event.

Reversed, The Hermit may point to unpleasant bouts of isolation and loneliness that should be tempered with some positive social time with supportive people. It may also indicate a refusal to learn or listen to advice, which can result in withdrawal from others in anger or resentment. It may be that you're prone to over-analysis and a tendency to intellectualize rather than allowing feelings to surface. Sometimes, looking too closely at a thing will prevent you from seeing it at all.

X
THE WHEEL OF FORTUNE

The Wheel of Fortune reminds us that seasons change and fortune fluctuates—nothing is permanent.

Change is one of its themes, along with luck, fate, karma, and joy. This card often appears in a reading concerning unexpected or unforeseen developments that change your plans or alter your course, for better or worse.

Whether you're in advantageous circumstances or in the midst of struggle, know that the Wheel is always turning—the most stable place to be is actually in the center, rather than on top or bottom. In that sense, this card may be advising you not to get stuck on particular plans at this time. No one is ever completely in control of events.

Upright, The Wheel of Fortune generally points to positive turns of events, whether happening presently or somewhere on the horizon. You will benefit from spontaneous success and joy as circumstances change unexpectedly for the better. This could manifest in a variety of ways, such as a suddenly appearing new career or a financial windfall.

Reversed, the card indicates a downturn in luck due to negative external forces over which you have little or no control. Unfortunately, you may have little influence over events at this time, but the situation will not prevail. This card is gently reminding you that everything—the good and the bad—is temporary.

XI
JUSTICE

If The Wheel of Fortune reminds us that we ultimately don't control circumstances, the Justice card reminds us that actions do have consequences. This is the card of truth, right judgment, resolution, and dealings with the law.

Justice teaches us about cause and effect, and may appear in a reading when you are trying to understand the role of destiny in your life. How much of what happens is connected to destiny, and how much is your own karma? As the Justice card is under the sign of Libra, paying attention to balance is also indicated. We are impacted by the decisions of others as much as we are by our own.

Upright, the Justice card points to the favorable conclusion of a dispute or other ongoing concern (provided that your success is deserved). It signals the importance of a reasoned, pragmatic approach to challenges as opposed to avoidance and denial, or extreme responses. Often, the present has to evolve before a clear understanding of the circumstances can emerge.

When the card is reversed, it can stand for dishonesty, unfairness and lack of accountability. A decision is made that is not in your favor, or a straightforward situation becomes unnecessarily complicated. Alternatively, in focusing on the unfair actions of some, you may be overlooking those who can support you at this difficult time. Remember to judge yourself kindly and hold fast to your beliefs.

XII
THE HANGED MAN

The Hanged Man is considered one of the most important figures in the spiritual journey of the soul. At times, we feel overwhelmed by circumstances and cannot see a way forward. The Hanged man represents waiting, letting go, and sacrifice, but also the ultimate rewards of salvation earned through a change of perspective.

It's important to note that the figure in this card is not being killed, but rather held literally in suspense. This card acknowledges that the greatest insights often follow periods of great trial, and that there is value in the time spent between difficulty and release.

Upright, The Hanged Man signifies the need for a time out. A situation that causes a feeling of "stuckness" is an opportunity to step back and get fresh insight and perspective. You may need to give up a particular belief or dream in order to be open to new understanding. You may be waiting for someone else to make a decision, unable to make your move until it happens. Don't waste energy fretting about what you are powerless to change. Trust that in time, you will have what you need to move forward again.

Reversed, the Hanged Man may indicate that it is you who is causing the immobility. You may be avoiding making a life-changing decision for fear of the initial discomfort it will cause. Fear of change is very powerful, even when we know the change will ultimately lead to better circumstances. Beware of betraying yourself in the effort to stay in your comfort zone.

XIII
DEATH

Perhaps the most commonly misunderstood card in the Tarot is the Death card. Almost never about literal death, this card is instead associated with change, endings and beginnings, resolution, and reflection.

Death may appear in a reading when a situation is naturally ending, reminding us to let go of what is dead or useless, the way a tree will shed its leaves to make room for the new growth that will eventually manifest. Another appropriate symbol for this card is the mythical Phoenix, who cyclically rises from the ashes of its own demise. This card follows The Hanged Man as the soul learns to let go of the old in preparation for the new.

Upright, the Death card often points to endings, whether it's a relationship, a job, or even an era in one's life. Change and transition are indicated here, and you are advised to understand and accept that this is necessary change. When you let go of the old, new people and opportunities are free to enter your world. It is better to embrace change than resist it. The Death card very often represents a blessing in disguise.

The Death card reversed usually indicates an inability to move on from a certain situation due to a fierce resistance to change. You may be living in the past more than you realize.

New growth is unavailable to you until you let go of whatever no longer represents who you are (or want to be). Take steps to release what has ended so that new opportunities can take root.

XIV
TEMPERANCE

The Temperance card represents the needs that arise as we work to incorporate our new growth into our lives.

Having experienced extremes of all kinds in the realms of emotion and attitudes, we eventually come to value balance. This is the card of transformation, reconciliation, and hope. Temperance mixes the inner world of the psyche with the external physical world and helps us appreciate the connectedness of all things. This card may appear in a reading to remind us that synchronicity of timing is available to all when we are still and balanced enough to recognize it.

Upright, Temperance points to the need for moderation, patience, and balance as a means of controlling the volatile influences and opposing demands in life. You are in a good place to use your experience to harmonize conflicts. When you do, there is potential for great progress in a relationship, business, or project. Temperance is the key to keeping positive influences in forward motion.

On the contrary, when the card is reversed, it can signal an imbalance, a lack of long term vision, and/or a tendency toward excess in general. You may feel overwhelmed, under pressure, or unfairly burdened by the demands of others. Do what you can to balance your responses to external issues in a healthy way. If money problems are involved, deal with them responsibly before they get worse.

XV
THE DEVIL

Another often misunderstood card, The Devil is not about the source of all evil in Christian myth, but the inner wildness we all possess that generally needs tempering (through the skills associated with the previous card).

The Devil is associated with temptation, addiction, and selfishness, but also with clouded perceptions that arise from enslavement to outmoded ideals. This card may appear in a reading to tell us that we're missing something important in the big picture, and that we must face our ignorance, our fears, and our limitations. These limitations can be caused by both too much and too little

Upright, The Devil may be indicating misdirected passion, such as an unhealthy love affair or an obsession with power and money. You may be allowing your baser instincts (lust, greed, the urge for power) to rule. Beware of investing energy or money in the wrong person or project for short-term gain. Alternatively, you may actually be neglecting your inner wild side too much. If you have too tight a reign on your behavior, you may be starving your creative powers. Either way, examine your current circumstances and your motives carefully, and avoid big decisions until you can see clearly again.

When The Devil is reversed, the implications may be more severe. Obsession, such as an unhappy destructive affair, or a struggle with addiction may by severely hampering you or someone in your life. The Devil reversed shows an inability or unwillingness to break a bond that has no future, due to immaturity, desperation, or low self-esteem. You need to understand the extent of your bondage before you can begin to see a way out.

XVI
THE TOWER

The Tower card signals transformation, the shattering of illusion, and sudden change. This kind of transformation is abrupt and may be unsettling or even downright frightening.

The Tower is associated with disaster, surrender, sudden endings, and egotism. It may mark the loss of a position or some other change with enormous implications. However, a literal event is not always indicated. The real meaning in this card is in the shattering of old constructs as the light of truth and higher consciousness prevails. Those at the highest points of realities created under false pretenses have the furthest to fall.

Upright, The Tower can be read as a sudden shock or loss that creates great insecurity: the collapse of an ideal or a relationship. What you have fabricated falls down, and there is little you can do to avoid the situation or repair it. But you will gain new wisdom from the situation, which you can use in the future. When this card appears, it's always good to remember the old saying: "Whatever doesn't kill you makes you stronger."

The Tower reversed can point to an avoidable disaster that is at least somewhat of your own making. Fear of change, resistance, dishonesty, or willful oblivion may be aggravating a situation and placing you in danger of losing everything. Do what you can if there's still time. If not, you will at least have the experience of seeing your worst fears realized and learning that life does go on. No matter what happens, a current struggle will have come to an end.

XVII
THE STAR

The Star appears in the Fool's journey as the calm after the storm kicked up in the events of The Tower card. After the disillusionment comes new clarity, and a breakthrough arises, or an opportunity suddenly becomes available.

The Star card is associated with guidance, inspiration, rewards, energy, and alignment with the creative source. While the significance of this card in a reading may relate to past events, the focus is on the future, and faith in the journey as we awaken to the larger patterns of meaning in the Universe.

When The Star is upright, it indicates an increased level of inspiration, spirituality, hope, and serenity. You have clarity of purpose and great potential now. You have reached a point where your past experiences enable you to make a dream come true. You are on the right path, using your creativity to cultivate success and happiness.

When The Star is reversed, discouragement may be indicated, as well as despair and general lack of faith. A creative or emotional block occurs as something you've been tending loses steam. You need direction, but you may not have been listening to the right people. Get back in touch with your inner guidance, and ask for help from those you trust at the gut level.

XVIII
THE MOON

The Moon card is one of the more mysterious of the Major Arcana, as it deals with illusion as well as psychic knowledge. Associated with the watery sign of Pisces, the Moon relates to the collective unconscious, as well as our dreams and intuition.

This card may appear in a reading to remind us that just as people can be unknowingly physically and emotionally affected by the energies of the full and new moons, we are subject to invisible forces that we can only partially sense. This card may appear in the context of psychic awakenings, difficult decisions, or crises of faith.

Upright, The Moon may be indicating a dilemma that troubles the subconscious and plays on personal insecurities. It is hard to know where to go from here. The Moon provides light as reflected from the Sun, but this light can only partially illuminate our path. Pay attention to your dreams, as well as any signs and signals in the exterior world that resonate with you, and be patient as you seek clarity. It may not yet be time to act, but to closely examine your options, and honor your intuition as you wait for further information.

When The Moon is reversed, it indicates an inability to honor your intuition. You may not trust your feelings at all and depend entirely on others for answers. However, this can be just as dangerous as acting from your own incorrect instinct, as others may have motives you're unaware of. Moonlight can be deceptive, and there may be just too much psychic debris in the air for you to see anything clearly at all at this time.

XIX
THE SUN

The Sun is the card of enlightenment, as we are granted time to bask in the successes of our journey thus far. This card is associated with victory, achievement, and joy, as well as recuperation, vitality, and growth. It represents the dawn of a new day after the worst and darkest night, the source of life and optimism.

The Sun is also associated with the dawn of the inner light of each soul on the spiritual quest. Another meaning relates to intellect, practicality, and power, as the physical sun is the source of all growth on Earth. It is said that this card has no truly severe indications—all is well, or soon will be, when The Sun appears.

Upright, The Sun points to positivity, success, upcoming fun and warmth. It is time for the good things in life: love, play, rest, and bright cheer. It may also indicate children coming into your life. It is not so much about swift forward motion as it is a moment to appreciate where you are. You are still growing, and it's important to appreciate times of rest and feelings of security.

If The Sun is reversed, you may not be feeling so positive just yet. There is a sense of delay or frustration, as your goal is just out of reach. However, just as the sun goes behind the clouds, it will come out again. Be sure not to focus on the gray, as it is always temporary. Trust that the feeling of joy, success, and easy rest will come again.

XX
JUDGEMENT

As the Fool's journey draws near the close, the Judgment card appears.

This is a time to review where we have been and make conscious decisions about the future, based on what we have learned. Judgment is associated with truth, renewal, forgiveness, freedom and higher consciousness. Its planet is Pluto, who rules the Underworld, suggesting the final review of the life of the soul as it passes from this world to the next. What do we need to forgive in ourselves or others? What will we take with us into the future, and what will we let go of?

Upright, the Judgment card points to rebirth, absolution and inner callings toward a higher level of being. A significant life change may be occurring as a project or relationship moves toward a conclusion. This may be a time to examine your conscience and review your previous actions. Judgment offers second chances and an opportunity for forgiveness. Another possible meaning is reward for past efforts that will help your future success. This card generally indicates the arrival of improved conditions.

When the card is reversed, the past may be getting in the way of moving forward. You may be refusing to examine your own role in your circumstances, or else judging yourself too harshly without the follow-up of self-forgiveness. Alternatively, others may be judging you unfairly and you may not know how to stand up for yourself. You may need help with moving past guilt over what cannot be undone. Absolution and renewal can only occur after you let go.

XXI
THE WORLD

The World card represents the triumphant conclusion of the spiritual journey. This card is associated with celebrations, completion, success, and reward, as well as the promise of new beginnings.

The path to inner peace and liberation is clearly illuminated when The World appears, as we see the interconnectedness of the self with all of creation. This card represents the achievement of whatever goal is being sought. Of course, the spiritual journey is cyclical, so there will be a new starting point for the soul to embark from, but for now, it is time to relish in the happy ending.

Upright, The World stands for integration, accomplishment, and happiness; a dream come true. Whatever your goal, you will achieve it and feel satisfied and rewarded. Celebration is called for in this time of joy, as a project is concluded or a difficult dilemma has been resolved. As a side note, The World may indicate that travel is on the horizon.

Reversed, The World can signify a lack of closure and completion. There is a sense of restriction and a failure to move forward, often as a result of indecision or negativity. You may need to address what is holding you back, whether it's your own attitudes or a tendency to be ruled by the needs of others, before you can get on track to realize your goal.

THE CARDS OF THE
MINOR ARCANA

THE SUIT OF WANDS

Also known as Batons, Clubs, Staves, Rods, Scepters, Spears, Arrows, this is the suit of inspiration, intention, and ambition. When we are feeling creative, inspired, spurred to action, and/or envisioning outcomes we are utilizing Wand energy.

Wands symbolize a desire to grow, expand, create, and take risks in order to make things happen. However, this energy is primarily in the *thought* as opposed to the corresponding *action*, so the potential drawback of Wands is that there's plenty of enthusiasm but not enough follow-through. If many Wands appear in a reading, this is an indication that things are either just beginning, or are still in the realm of ideas, not yet manifest.

Wands also point to what we desire and what we fear, since these two feelings are usually the source of our motivations. While the qualities of passion and energy associated with initiative understandably lead some systems to assign Wands to the element of Fire, the correspondence with Air in Wiccan traditions emphasizes the realm of thought, ideas, and inspiration.

Key words most often used in association with Wands: new ideas, ambition, new ventures, inspiration, enthusiasm, growth, expansion.

ACE OF WANDS

Upright: inspiration, good communication, potential, new beginnings, creative success.

The Ace of Wands predicts success in all kinds of new plans and projects. This is a very good time to take an important step forward. If you're uncertain about how to proceed with an idea or inspiration, the Ace is advising you to take a risk and go for whatever it is you truly want to do.

Reversed: Lack of motion, delays.

The right timing for pursuing your creative goal is not here yet. It may be difficult to seek cooperation from others or to get what you need to move forward. You may experience frustration due to delayed projects or activities like travel or special events. Success is still indicated ultimately, but only with patience.

TWO OF WANDS

Upright: Progress, planning the future, discovery, decisions, a reliable partner.

Conditions are favorable for assistance and progress in partnerships, equality and financial security. New discoveries will be encouraging, and your efforts will bring stability and will be worthwhile.

Reversed: Lack of planning, fear of the unknown, inequality.

In a partnership, one person has more influence or input than the other. There may be an imbalance of work load or a financial inequality causing difficulties with progress. If you are facing a decision alone, then one part of you is at odds with another regarding whether to move forward in a new direction. Examine what you think you stand to lose if you forge ahead.

THREE OF WANDS

Upright: Foresight, expansion, preparation, enterprise, self-expression, creativity.

In the development of projects, events speed up, communication and action increase, and money flows your way. Your efforts are working, particularly when they involve more creative approaches to solving problems.

Reversed: Delays, lack of foresight, obstacles, misconception.

Misunderstandings between people (usually groups of at least three) where progress is halted instead of moving toward intended goals. Stay as neutral as you can and avoid direct confrontations during this time. Adaptation to change is crucial.

FOUR OF WANDS

Upright: Harmony, celebrations, home, satisfaction.

Four of Wands usually reflects positivity and harmony, while spreading positive feelings and positive results. You're in a good, satisfied place now, bringing together different elements of your life and getting more joy out of them. Matters of reinvention of the home may come up and are more able to be realized now. Appreciate what you have.

Reversed: Transition, postponement, a break in communication.

There may be elements of your life in conflict that are proving hard to harmonize. Resistance from others or from external forces keep your goals just out of reach. Stay focused and open rather than jumping to accept defeat.

FIVE OF WANDS

Upright: Competition, disagreement, tension, strife, conflict, diligence, a test.

Now is a time to pay attention to details and stay awake to potential complications in your endeavors. You need to be prepared for struggle, and to fight for what you hold to be important.

Reversed: Diversity, avoiding conflict, agreeing to disagree, deception.

You may feel wronged or misled or witness others experiencing this kind of conflict. You may feel you have not deserved some current circumstances brought about by the decisions of others. Stay out of resentment as much as you can—it doesn't help move things forward.

SIX OF WANDS

Upright: Victory, success, public recognition, self-confidence, progress, reward.

Obstacles are overcome and a breakthrough of some kind is imminent. The Six of Wands focuses on good news, success and completion of tasks at hand. It may feel like moving forward after being temporarily stalled. Six is good for resolving legal matters, delayed contracts, or a work issue. You succeed, and your reward is well deserved. Time to celebrate!

Reversed: Disrepute, a fall from grace, egotism, lack of confidence, disappointment.

Reward has eluded you. You experience general delays to plans, and/or feelings of suspicion and frustration. There is a potential for feeling exclusion, confusion, or insecurity. Examine what went wrong and learn from it for next time.

SEVEN OF WANDS

Upright: Competition, challenge, perseverance, strength.

Your goals are worth pursuing, no matter that the way might not be easy. Perseverance gets you where you need to be. You may need to sustain faith over a long stretch of time before you see results, but chances are very good that you will.

Reversed: Being overwhelmed, giving up, resistance, a communication barrier.

You may be at a dead end in a situation involving communications / negotiations with others. Some obstacle involving conflicting viewpoints and yours is not being heard/taken into account. Sometimes you have to let go and save your efforts for a more favorable endeavor later on.

EIGHT OF WANDS

Upright: Action, speed, travel, swift changes, movement, opportunities.

You receive unexpected good news, generally about a trip or project. The eight signals an active time with plenty of forward movement. Your contributions are recognized and you feel valued and able to connect with others who share your goals.

Reversed: Frustration, delays, holding off, discernment.

You may be unsure about one or more opportunities currently under consideration. Listen to your gut if there seems to be too much risk of wasted energy. It might be hard to get access to genuinely solid opportunities at the moment. Beware of making rash or hasty decisions.

NINE OF WANDS

Upright: Persistence, courage, resilience, a test of faith, resourcefulness.

There's a lot of activity now; you are busy and under pressure, but capable of getting things done and keeping sane, clear, and sufficiently energized. Accept the current pace and go with the flow of accelerated and hard work, rather than getting snagged in stress or resistance. Discipline and order will pay off.

Reversed: Defensiveness, paranoia, hesitation, pressure.

You are likely at full capacity and can't take on anything more at this time. Frayed nerves will start to show and you'll need to take care of yourself. Put off important decisions until you have more energy.

TEN OF WANDS

Upright: Responsibility, a burden, stress, hard work, achievement.

There's a lot on your plate and on your shoulders, and some of it is likely related to past decisions. It's hard to move forward or see your way clearly to your destination as you verge on overwhelm (or reach it). You may need time to work through a few things and/or let the dust settle before you achieve your goal. Early in a reading, this card signals that right now might not be the best time for divination work. You might do better to wait and try again later.

Reversed: Avoiding responsibility, over-burdening, self-deception.

You may be struggling with your circumstances in how much you've taken on, but mistakenly blaming others for your decisions. Your perspective might be off at this time due to stress. Stay out of blame and victim mentality. Ultimately, you'll end up with a lighter load if you keep your head down and plod along now.

PAGE OF WANDS

Upright: Exploration, enthusiasm, discovery, cautious progress.

This is generally a card of good news, and indicates that you may have several important things to pay attention to. The Page is a messenger and brings encouragement about new ideas. However, beware of unbridled enthusiasm: check the facts for yourself rather than taking someone's word for it. This energy is social and loves to talk, but is also flighty. Beware of rumors and resist gossip.

Reversed: Pessimism, setbacks, manipulation, lack of direction.

Gossip or malicious talk may be circulating as someone stands to benefit from it, even if it's just for entertainment. This energy is shallow and enjoys stirring things up. Don't take anything at face value and don't expect that you have all the necessary information to get at the truth of a situation.

KNIGHT OF WANDS

Upright: Passion, energy, action, adventure, creativity, success.

This is an inspiring and creative time, and what you have been seeking is starting to materialize, whether it's a project or even a person. The Knight is always looking forward, with spirit and determination. Things are likely to be speeding up now, as what you need for success falls into place.

Reversed: Scattered energy, impulsiveness, frustration, delays, insincerity.

This is a warning about the dangers of talk without substance, particularly on the part of others. This energy is enthusiastic but insincerely so, in that no effort will be made to support your endeavors. Watch out for people or situations that are likely to be far less helpful than you may be led to believe.

QUEEN OF WANDS

Upright: Warmth, exuberance, determination, vibrance, inspiration, passion.

This Queen has the qualities of creativity, clarity, and integrity, and inspires those around her. She is a thoughtful hard worker, independent, self-assured, and honest. This energy is sensitive to the feelings of others and lends wisdom and support to others in their endeavors. A new, inspiring influence may be entering your life.

Reversed: Aggression, disinterest, neglect, unreliability.

The reversed Queen indicates that you may be let down by someone in your world, particularly if you've been led to believe you have support available in a project or responsibility. You may be succumbing to impatience or making unreasonable demands. Promises may be broken; beware of unreliable people at this time.

KING OF WANDS

Upright: Vision, a natural-born leader, honor, compassion, entrepreneur.

This energy is wise, calm and compassionate. This King doesn't make demands of others, but does share ideas and energy with those close to him. Honorable behavior is indicated here, with the related association of feeling comfortable in your own skin. You are respected and people enjoy your presence.

Reversed: Haste, impulsiveness, high expectations, ruthless, prejudice.

The reversed King reveals negative thoughts and attitudes, and this energy is one of intolerance and narrow-mindedness. This is the reality of the unexamined conscience, with no thought for the consequences of actions or regard for the opinions of others. There is a bitterness to this kind of person that is caused by long-held spiteful beliefs.

THE SUIT OF CUPS

Also known as Chalices, Bowls, Goblets, Vases, Bowls and even Hearts, this is the suit of emotion and intuition.

Once an idea or inspiration has occurred, we experience an inner response to it—this inner response will determine whether, and in what manner, action will be taken. When we respond emotionally to ideas, events, and environments, whether we communicate our response outwardly or not, we are in the energetic realm of Cups. Often we may not be consciously aware of our inner feelings regarding a situation, and may be complicating things with our unexamined responses.

Many Cups in a reading can signal that the main forces at play in our current circumstances are rooted in the emotional realm. Cups represent love, relationships, connectedness, and imagination. Joyful emotions are usually indicated, but there is also potential for sorrow.

In most divination systems, Cups are associated with the element of Water, which always takes on the form of whatever contains it, and follows the path of least resistance. For this reason, Cups warn us of being too open or lacking useful boundaries.

Key words most often used in association with Cups:
emotion, desire, inner experience, intuition, spirit.

ACE OF CUPS

Upright: Compassion, love, overwhelming or strong emotion.

The Ace of Cups demonstrates a fresh start of a passionate nature and indicates emotional fulfillment, creativity and contentment. From falling passionately in love with a person, or committing to following a spiritual or artistic calling, this is a time of bliss. Pregnancy or childbirth may also be indicated, as this is a card of ultimate femininity.

Reversed: Repressed or blocked emotions, stagnation.

An emotional block may prevent the growth of love, leading to stagnation and emptiness. There may be anxiety around having enough time or emotional energy to spend with loved ones. Problems with fertility may also be indicated.

TWO OF CUPS

Upright: Partnership, unified love, relationships, attraction.

The two indicates a happy relationship and/or a favorable promise, such as an engagement. This card also favors close friendships and creative teams and points to easy, quality communication. Reconciliation after a rift is also a likely outcome.

Reversed: A relationship imbalance, lack of harmony, separation.

In a partnership, one person may be unwilling to commit. Communication failures lead to jealousy or other divisions, and usually to break-ups. The revealing of secrets against one's will may destroy trust.

THREE OF CUPS

Upright: Friendship, celebrations, community, creativity, growth, healing.

A period of happiness and celebration. The three represents accomplishment and healing, connectedness and renewal of friendship. A relationship grows in strength, love grows, and creativity flourishes. Childbirth may be indicated or new projects may be taking shape. You feel rejuvenated, physically and emotionally. Spend some time appreciating the inherent beauty that surrounds you on a daily basis.

Reversed: An affair, stifled creativity, betrayal.

There is disappointment in a relationship; a partner or a close friend betrays fidelity or confidence. You may find yourself unable to rely on those you are accustomed to turning to for help. The reversed three can also indicate low energy and possible health problems.

FOUR OF CUPS

Upright: Contemplation, meditation, reevaluation, boredom.

Monotony may begin to manifest in a relationship. The phrase "the honeymoon phase" applies here, as after the excitement of something new wears off, there's an adjustment period of a new "normal" setting in. Bonds that aren't innately strong may fizzle out. This card also teaches that long-lasting relationships are built on more solid foundations than mere passion.

Reversed: A missed opportunity, being aloof, apathy.

The reversed four may indicate emotional burnout or feeling isolated/depressed, poor health or lack of self-esteem. A relationship may have become complacent or static. This is a time of apathy and fatigue, where nothing is fulfilling. Taking interest in something, no matter how seemingly insignificant, can help break up the monotony.

FIVE OF CUPS

Upright: Regret, loss, despair, disappointment, bereavement, unhappiness.

The 5 of any suit can be viewed as troublesome. Here it may indicate trusts that have been dashed or grieving over something that is lost. This may relate to unhappy relationships, whether romantic love or friendship. People become distant and are unable to reconnect. This card could appear if you have refused to move on from a past error, especially when it's blocking you from a brand new opportunity that you need to seize as soon as possible.

Letting go is advised here. Not every relationship is meant to last—we learn our lessons from each other and then move on.

Reversed: Acceptance, moving on, forgiveness, healing.

Emotional wounds are healing. A broken dream or heartbreak is being left behind and you are able to make room for new possibilities as time passes. The circumstances are no longer totally miserable, and you are able to start moving in a more extroverted direction again.

SIX OF CUPS

Upright: Nostalgia, reunion, innocence, fond memories, benefits of experience.

In this card the past is a positive influence, and you appreciate all you have learned and accomplished in earlier times. Old friends or acquaintances may brush back into your life, which offers you a fresh perspective on your present and brings hope for the future.

Reversed: Naivety, being stuck in the past, being unrealistic, sentimentality.

You may be stuck in the past and unable to accept present circumstances. You are unable to see current opportunities or take advantage of the chance to develop new relationships. Additionally, you may be in a particular partnership, romantic or otherwise, that seems to have no future.

SEVEN OF CUPS

Upright: Confusion, fantasy, choices, wishful thinking.

You may be unsure which of many possible directions to choose. You have many opportunities or invitations coming your way and you're aware that there is a lot of potential available for you to make the most of your abilities and talents, but not every possibility will provide the same potential. The card is an alert against over admiring your circumstance and getting your head lost among the mists. You need to rely on your intuition now and let both logic and fantasy take a back seat. The "obvious choice" may not actually be the best choice.

Reversed: Illusion, temptation, diversionary tactics or actions.

Your fantasies require a firm establishment so as to flourish. You may be too attached to a particular relationship, environment, or project, and are unable or unwilling to see potential problems. This can end up in disappointment once the full truth becomes too obvious to ignore. Trying to escape into false realities is not recommended.

EIGHT OF CUPS

Upright: Disappointment, withdrawal, abandonment, a change of heart.

An established relationship faces an important decision. Long-term thinking is important here, as at least one person is likely to want to move on. If this is you, weigh your options carefully beforehand, so you'll have confidence that you've made the right choice.

Reversed: Aimless drifting, hopelessness, escapism, poor judgment.

A relationship may be abandoned due to anxiety, wanderlust, and/or an unwillingness to work through problems, either personal or interpersonal. Positive opportunities are ignored in the desire for flight, which may be regretted later.

NINE OF CUPS

Upright: Fulfilled wishes, happiness, comfort, satisfaction.

The nine signals that wishes are being granted, particularly in relationships. Good news, good health, and emotional and financial security are indicated. That which you have been hoping for is or soon will be materializing.

Reversed: Dissatisfaction, greed, materialism, vanity.

Egotism wreaks havoc on love relationships or friendships and results in emotional wounding and disharmony. Either you or someone else is caught up in self-centeredness that injures and causes divisions. Alternatively, this card can also point to frustrating delays to plans.

TEN OF CUPS

Upright: Marriage, harmony, alignment, happiness, contentment.

A positive, blissful card for romance, friendship, and family relationships. The ten points to stability and enjoyment, satisfaction and a feeling of wholeness. Relationships and group activities are peaceful and harmonious. This card predicts bonding and happy togetherness, and occasions for reunion.

Reversed: Broken relationships, misalignment of values, distance.

Group activities don't fare well here, meaning possibly you are on your own more than you'd like. Disruption, temporary disharmony may arise in a family or other group, due to one person's actions.

PAGE OF CUPS

Upright: Creative beginnings, guidance.

This Page may bring good news about a relationship, or indicate a social and creative influence. There is a youthful energy around this time that favors expression through music or some other art. As part of the Cups suit, there is a dreaminess and possibly unfocused energy, which may point to the need to be more grounded in approach to romantic love. Additionally, you may be called upon to provide guidance to others.

Reversed: Creative block, emotional immaturity, frustration.

Reversed, the Page indicates a personality that has trouble with positive self-expression. An energy of immaturity is present, possibly in a child or adolescent in your life who is seeking attention but in negative ways. A situation may present what you feel to be unnecessary drama.

KNIGHT OF CUPS

Upright: Charm, romance, affection.

New relationships and new friends are likely on the way when this Knight appears. This is a celebratory energy that encourages sociability and gratitude for good times. If the situation involves romance, it may be short-lived, as this energy represents more of a temporary good time than a lasting phenomenon.

Reversed: Jealousy, impracticality, moodiness, emptiness.

The reversed Knight indicates a person whose words should be taken with a giant grain of salt. This is an energy of broken promises and deceit, with nothing to offer you. Don't believe any fantastical scenarios painted presented to you at this time.

QUEEN OF CUPS

Upright: Calm, emotional security, compassionate, intuitive, nurturing, insight.

This Queen is a natural caregiver with mature, maternal energy. Sensitive and insightful, she advises you to take care of yourself and others, and pay attention to what your intuition is telling you. This energy is about allowing the heart to lead the mind, which can be more useful than logic for solving certain mysteries. This may be a time to attend to your deeper needs.

Reversed: Co-dependency, emotional insecurity, jealousy, infidelity.

This energy is selfish in that it seeks attention from others; an emotional neediness that threatens to drain you. Avoid tendencies toward jealousy, but also be aware that someone may actually be being unfaithful, which this reversed queen arrives to warn you about.

KING OF CUPS

Upright: Generosity, emotional balance, problem-solving, intuition.

This King is a strong negotiator and quietly authoritative.

He may seem distant or lost in his own thoughts, but is a kind, supportive and wise presence. He indicates that problems will be solved and that your heart may be better suited than your head just now to assess a situation. This energy is calm, cooling, and reassuring.

Reversed: Moodiness, emotional manipulation, volatility, destructive behavior.

This energy is volatile emotionally, as unpredictable highs and lows wreak havoc all around. This card may indicate a person who avoids dealing with problems and exhibits destructive behavior due to fear of commitment.

THE SUIT OF SWORDS

Also known as Blades, Knives, Scimitars, Feathers and Arrows, Swords is the suit of *action*, which is the result of the combining of ideas (Wands) with emotions (Cups).

The effort involved in pursuing a goal, which can often be perceived as struggle, is the realm of Sword energy. It can be hard to turn our ideas into reality, but this is also where the most learning tends to occur.

Many Swords in a reading are likely reflecting a high level of activity or commotion in a current situation as it moves toward a final result. Swords are logical rather than emotional, and can therefore be cold or harsh with their messages, as they cut straight through any illusions we may be clinging to. Rationality is needed to solve problems, and detachment is often advised by the cards in this suit. In some cases, Swords may signify strength, authority, and power, as well as the more unfortunate elements of human nature that lead to violence and suffering.

While the qualities of logic and reason associated with problem solving understandably lead some systems to assign Swords to the element of Air, the correspondence with Fire in Wiccan traditions emphasizes the realm of action leading to transformation of reality.

Key words most often used in association with Swords: action, movement, struggle, shrewdness, responsibility.

ACE OF SWORDS

Upright: Victory, progress, raw power, mental clarity, break-throughs.

The ace of Swords predicts a strong level of activity that will lead to success. Although you may need mental acuity to withstand challenges, victory and progress prevail over opposition. This card symbolizes the faculty of thought and intellect, as well as justice. You may be making decisions on a bigger level, for which you will need a clear head.

Reversed: Loss, chaos, confusion, lack of clarity.

Loss, possibly failure is indicated. Delayed plans. If you're dwelling too much on what's not working, this can prevent you from being able to solve problems. Work on finding a new way forward rather than obsessing over being stuck. Beware of deception and/or confusion about big decisions.

TWO OF SWORDS

Upright: Choices, indecision, stalemate, truce.

After turmoil or disharmony, peace is restored, but it may be uncertain. Take advantage of the momentary calm to gain perspective on a troublesome partnership or association. Carefully consider every aspect of the situation and be willing to balance your needs with those of the other person or people involved.

Reversed: Confusion, indecision, informational overload, suspicion.

The two can point to doubt over decisions and giving into fear. There may be a lack of trust, possibly stemming from deception in a partnership. Others may prefer drama and manipulation to straightforward dealings. Be direct in your pursuit of answers.

THREE OF SWORDS

Upright: Sorrow, heartbreak, rejection, grief.

It's time to address a painful situation. This card indicates heartbreak, sorrow, and deep disappointment due to the loss of a relationship or an ideal. Accept the situation, knowing that something better will emerge in its place.

Reversed: struggle, chaos.

Drama and upheaval. You are struggling to get out of a relationship or commitment that has not turned out the way you had perceived. Chaos may be a result of this situation, but it will ultimately pass.

FOUR OF SWORDS

Upright: Recovery, contemplation, relaxation, passivity, rest.

After a time of intense activity and/or pressure, there is a period of calm and recovery. The four symbolizes the rest after a difficult challenge, especially when you need it, so that you can figure out things and recover before finally going back to the challenge that has been bothering you and causing you issues. Recuperation from illness may also be indicated.

Reversed: Burn-out, illness, avoidance, disruption.

This may be a time of brief illness or other interruption from the normal day-to-day life. You may feel isolated from others for circumstantial reasons. This card can also indicate a problematic habit of setting problems aside in order to evade them. Don't allow yourself to stay down for too long—you'll need to get back in the game and pick up where you left off eventually.

FIVE OF SWORDS

Upright: Tension, conflict, loss, wanting to win at all costs, defeat, betrayal.

This card suggests that the current problem you face doesn't have a viable solution and that you may be wasting energy trying to succeed. It's time to find a way to leave the situation, admit defeat and move on. Continuing to struggle only makes things worse. As a side note, debt and/or poverty may be indicated, so be careful not to exhaust your financial or energetic reserves. "Choose your battles wisely" is a good adage to live by when the five appears.

Reversed: Past resentment, exposure.

Rather than admitting defeat, you may be clinging to the hope of victory and be in denial about where things truly stand. You are afraid to admit to past mistakes because you don't want to be criticized. Things are likely to only get worse if you continue in this vein. It may be a painful blow to the ego, but it's best to own up to your mistakes now, and/or admit that you've been betrayed.

SIX OF SWORDS

Upright: a necessary transition, peace restored.

After possibly a long period of difficulty, harmony is restored and you can take some time away from the commotion. Things may not be completed, but a break is available to you at this time. Take advantage of it and you'll return to your work with renewed energy.

Reversed: Carrying baggage, the inability to move on, enforced delay.

You may be dealing with stagnation, depletion, and a lack of focus. You'd like a break, but now is not the time: you must keep going, or you will lose out on valuable opportunities. Gather your strength and push forward, or you may risk losing all you've worked for up to this point.

SEVEN OF SWORDS

Upright: dispossession, cunning, stealth.

There may be someone in a situation who wants something from you. Be on your toes about this and keep an eye on your personal possessions at this time. There's a lack of trust in the situation and you will need to use your wits to triumph.

Reversed: deception, dishonesty.

The reversed position indicates even higher likelihood of

theft or other dishonest behavior. Pay attention to hidden motives on the part of others. You may be feeling bullied or pressured and more inclined to give in than to fight back. You are advised to summon your courage and stand up for yourself.

EIGHT OF SWORDS

Upright: isolation, imprisonment, denial.

A project or relationship is failing and you feel unable to repair it. You lack energy and strength for facing up to the situation and would rather be in denial. You need to work your way out of emotional lethargy. Find help if you can, but do whatever it takes to break free.

Reversed: self-imposed restriction, self-blame.

You are blaming yourself for recent events, making it impossible to move forward into more positive circumstances. You are too caught up in guilt and self-reproach to see your way out of the problem. Don't use up your energy on a situation you can't change. Instead, focus on finding your way out.

NINE OF SWORDS

Upright: Nightmares, severe depression, intense anxiety, suffering, victimization.

You may be on the verge of falling apart due to stress and anxiety. There may be constant battle going on at this time that threatens your health. Some element of your life has been very difficult lately. It will take strength and patience, but you will get through this challenging time.

Reversed: Severe depression, hopelessness, torment, martyrdom.

You may be so full of despair that you can't see anything positive about anything at the moment. This card arises when your response to a difficult situation gets overblown and you become hopeless and attached to a victim role. Beware of getting used to this way of thinking and feeling, as it will prevent you from moving forward. Do what you can to get an objective look at the issues.

TEN OF SWORDS

Upright: Defeat, loss, endings.

The ten is about endings with a view toward new beginnings. In the Swords suit, endings can be dramatic or harsh, but you will move past it more easily than it may appear. The situation is finally over and truth has come to light. Whatever has ended needed to end, in order to provide room for new opportunities coming your way.

Reversed: Regeneration, recovery, an inevitable end, fear of ruin.

When reversed, the ten is more often about group dynamics than individuals. This card may point to the end of a situation involving a group, such as a particular set of colleagues in a work environment or a group of friends. This ending is not welcomed, but it's best to view it as positively as you can. Together you can help each other see the silver linings.

PAGE OF SWORDS

Upright: Curiosity, intelligence, perception.

This Page brings helpful, practical advice. He is also an astute judge of character, and indicates that you will need your wits about you in order to successfully navigate a situation. Intelligence is key and a helpful mentor may come your way in this regard.

Reversed: Gullibility, undelivered promises, mischief.

Deception is a possibility here. It's hard to know where you are and/or to ascertain the truth about a situation. Keep your eyes peeled for subtle misinformation intentionally thrown your way, or important information withheld, and consider new agreements very carefully.

KNIGHT OF SWORDS

Upright: Haste, action, a battle.

This King indicates that a future battle will be necessary to resolve a problem. This is a force that's usually temporary in your life, but it's very energetic and it boosts courage, so you know you will prevail. Watch out for the tendency to rush into action without first considering the consequences.

Reversed: Disregard for consequences, impatience, false heroics.

This energy is potentially manipulative, and enjoys chaos for the sake of chaos. Conflict is indicated. Someone around you at the moment is unreliable, and may exit the situation after stirring it up, leaving you to deal with the mess.

QUEEN OF SWORDS

Upright: Organization, perception, independence, eloquence.

This Queen displays the qualities of intelligence, eloquence, and loyalty, but only to a certain extent. This energy is charming, but protective of its interests. She will not put anyone else's needs in front of her own, particularly when it comes to business. You may be getting temporary help from someone in this energetic realm if your goals are compatible with theirs.

Reversed: Moodiness, ruthlessness.

The reversed Queen is a piercing force of negativity. This energy is self-obsessed and often cruel, and as a situation, indicates that you will lose out in a negotiation. This energy does not care about the feelings of others, and it is unfortunate to be under her rule.

KING OF SWORDS

Upright: Intellect, clear thinking, authority, truth, ambition.

This King's energy is about strategy and problem solving, seeing the big picture and knowing how to delegate. This card is favorable for the start of projects, but also a reminder to pay attention to the details for more efficient success. Use logic, insight, and discipline to the best of your ability.

Reversed: Tyranny, manipulation, cruelty.

This King is a harsh energy who ruthlessly and relentlessly pursues his goals. Winning is more important than kindness and he has no problem being cruel if it gets him what he wants. If you are dealing with a tyrannical person, it's best to get out of the way as much as possible. In a project, expect opposition and even confrontation.

THE SUIT OF PENTACLES

Also known as Coins, Stones, Disks, Circles, Shields, and Talismans, this is the suit of manifestation. Pentacles represent the result of inspiration which is responded to and acted upon.

As opposed to thoughts, emotions, or actions, the energetic realm of Pentacles is more associated with mastery of the material plane. While often relating to matters of home and money, they also speak to issues around tradition, control, and/or power, along with the physical body.

When many Pentacles appear in a reading, the indication is that some kind of result is either taking shape presently or already manifest. Many of the cards relate to rewards for hard work, while others may highlight fears around material insecurity.

In most divination systems, Pentacles are associated with the element of Earth, as they relate to abundance, security, and the importance of being grounded in material reality. They remind us to keep our feet on the ground and appreciate the physical experience of being alive.

Key words most often used in association with Pentacles: manifestation, realization, fruition, proof, prosperity, security, reward.

ACE OF PENTACLES

Upright: material success, manifestation, prosperity.

The Ace of this suit indicates new opportunities for financial gain. Money may also come in the form of unexpected gifts, prizes, or investments (as opposed to earned income). You will likely be relieved by complete material security and reassurance after uncertainty about resources. This is an auspicious time for new businesses and relationships—a comfortable, prosperous time.

Reversed: Lack of planning, lost opportunity, financial loss.

Reversed, this card warns of potential problems with money—either your own overspending, or greed on the part of others. This is not a time to take risks with anything you want to hang onto. As a side meaning, the reversed Ace may also indicate a relationship based on Materialism rather than love.

TWO OF PENTACLES

Upright: Adaptability, balance, time management, solvency.

You may be in uncertain times concerning money, but if you are responsible and careful, you will be fine. In the midst of busy and unpredictable circumstances, have faith in your material well-being and your ability to juggle responsibilities. As a side note, be sure you are pulling your weight around the house so as not to be a burden on others.

Reversed: Financial disarray, disorganization, money worries.

There may be a problem with a business or romantic partner over money. There may be dishonesty at play in the business world or funds may be low, leading to a higher sense of risk. This may be a dangerous time. Keep your wits about you and avoid excesses of spending or imbalanced behavior.

THREE OF PENTACLES

Upright: creativity, teamwork.

This card points to success for those making their way in the business world or who create and sell their own goods. Mastery in specific skills is indicated. Pride and achievement are celebrated now as you see your creative abilities strengthened and smoothly flowing. This may involve a new home or business location, or simply an upswing in your enthusiasm and productivity. You may also rise in rank or status among your peers.

Reversed: creative block, lack of teamwork.

There is an element of denial getting in the way of creative progress. Work is being neglected due to over-fantasizing about the ultimate vision for a project. Either you or someone else needs to come back down to earth and get busy. Watch out for sloppiness that results in lower-quality outcomes, banal ideas, or a general inability to stop focusing on things that really have no value.

This may be related to efforts to acquire property, which may be delayed at this time.

FOUR OF PENTACLES

Upright: Stability, confidence, security.

The four indicates stability and firm foundations. What you have been working for is secured and you can move forward with confidence and assurance after a period of uncertainty. Whether it's a project, a business, or an educational endeavor, success is predicted. Recovery from health issues is also indicated.

Reversed: Materialism, greed, self-protection, limitation.

You may feel undervalued and/or left out of success, perceiving that you can't achieve rewards for your efforts. Continuing in this mindset will likely keep you from seeing new opportunities where your abilities will be better recognized. Don't let temporary setbacks get in the way of your focus on a positive future. Beware of a "miserly" attitude toward material success.

FIVE OF PENTACLES

Upright: Insecurity, isolation, financial loss, worry, poverty, hardship.

The five upsets the stability of the four, indicating either financial hardship or simply a strong fear of poverty. You may feel like you're missing out on the fun because of low funds. You may simply be losing faith as it seems something difficult is on the horizon. Don't let poverty-consciousness get the best of you, however—things will look up and you'll be able to prevent further falling into the negative.

Reversed: Spiritual poverty, recovery from a financial loss, greed.

Money problems are potentially severe when the five is reversed, and security and partnerships may be at risk. Greed and poor judgment have led to dire straits, and the fault lies with you or someone close to you, rather than in external circumstances. Accept where you are in the moment and begin planning to work your way out of the mess. Seek help when it is needed and try not to fear rejection.

SIX OF PENTACLES

Upright: Charity, generosity, a gift, prosperity.

You may receive a windfall of some kind, whether it's simple appreciation from a friend or business associate, or an unexpected bonus or other payout. You may also be inspired to be generous to someone else—a person or a worthy cause.

Reversed: Selfishness, debt, one-sided charity, meanness.

You may be either offered a bad deal or denied something that is owed to you. When people get worried about there being enough to go around, tensions flare up. A spirit of bad faith is in the air, so avoid relying on others to be true to their word at this time.

SEVEN OF PENTACLES

Upright: Perseverance, vision, reward, profit, investment.

The seven is always a message about faith in the long term outcome of your efforts. There is great potential for you to achieve your material goals, whether it's professional development/education, a new home, or something else. You have what you need, but you will need to sustain effort and determination, as this is just the beginning. Resist thinking you should change course in moments of doubt—stay on the path you've chosen. If it seems hard to see the benefit, focus on the spiritual and emotional rewards of the extra work that you're putting in.

Reversed: Limited success, lack of vision for the long-term, limited reward, procrastination.

Worry over money or other security threatens to blind you into giving up. This card advises you to take action rather than sitting around hoping it will go away. Problems are often much bigger before we take a close look at them. Don't let anxiety keep you from taking steps to solve the crisis at hand.

EIGHT OF PENTACLES

Upright: Education, apprenticeship, engagement, quality, opportunity.

This card points to areas of commission, craftsmanship, work, and skills in a specific craft or business. The eight indicates that an opportunity is coming your way that brings material reward. You are advised to accept, as you will see your needs met by this endeavor, whether it's a small project or an educational advancement. Invest in yourself now and you will see it pay off.

Reversed: Lack of ambition, perfectionism, over commitment.

You may feel trapped by a commitment that zaps your time, money, and/or energy. Do what you can to reconcile the situation; it's better to bow out than to sacrifice what would be better to put into a more favorable endeavor.

NINE OF PENTACLES

Upright: Luxury, gratitude, culmination, self-sufficiency, order, pleasure.

The nine is often about restoring order or harmony, and in this suit it indicates that disputes or issues relating to the home—family, neighbors, or the building itself—are now resolving. This card may signal a time when you can treat yourself to luxury. Money woes are over and financial security rules. This is a good time to appreciate all that you have, particularly in the home.

Reversed: Financial setbacks, money wars.

Serious money problems jeopardize your home and/or security. Arguments about finances are straining relationships. One person may be overly dependent on another for material needs. You need to try to find perspective and start putting out the fire before it spreads.

TEN OF PENTACLES

Upright: Inheritance, wealth, establishment, family, retirement, happiness.

As the ultimate card of Pentacles, the ten focuses on family and generations. It can predict a happy marriage and children, or financial benefits arising from inheritance or generous friends or relatives. It is a favorable card for families, both in present times and in future outlook.

Reversed: Loneliness, financial failure, loss, family conflict.

Reversed, the ten points to conflict within the family, usually over money issues, perhaps relating to wills and inheritance, or other long-term expectations that don't come to fruition. It could also point to inter-generational strife as belief systems differ between older and younger family members.

PAGE OF PENTACLES

Upright: Financial opportunity, manifestation, a new job.

The Page represents hard work, maturity, diligence. This energy favors new projects but advises you to stay on top of financial concerns, avoiding wasteful spending in order to be in good shape down the road. Don't over-indulge just because things are going well.

Reversed: Lack of planning, lack of progress, short-term focus, irresponsibility.

This energy is reckless, revealing that someone is likely overspending and affecting your financial situation. You may find you need to slow down in order to get back on track again. Funding problems that delay projects may also be indicated.

KNIGHT OF PENTACLES

Upright: Routine, efficiency, security, progress.

Energy and a sense of purpose are applied to projects and financial matters. This Knight is reliable and grounded, signifying steady progress in a favorable direction. On the flip side, if you tend to be set in your ways, this card may be advising you to loosen up a little.

Reversed: Boredom, laziness, inaction, dishonesty.

The reversed Knight may be a schemer who attempts to get you to do his work for him. This energy is not interested in getting ahead through inspiration and hard work, but would rather someone else fix the problem. Avoid trusting in someone who seems to be all talk and no action, and avoid succumbing to procrastination.

QUEEN OF PENTACLES

Upright: Practicality, security, generosity.

This Queen is mature, generous and grounded, offering wisdom, support and stability in finances as well as emotions. She may be a business woman of some kind, a provider, a patron of the arts, or someone who embodies the ideals of working hard to reach success. This is a positive card predicting happiness.

Reversed: An imbalance in familial commitments, an imbalance in work, miserliness.

Reversed, this energy is withholding of money and /or support, and indicates insecurity and lack of trust. This Queen has no interest in the welfare of others. She may be wealthy, but she's miserable for all the worry she feels over the possibility of loss. You may be being advised to avoid someone like this, or simply to be thrifty yourself for a while.

KING OF PENTACLES

Upright: security, abundance, discipline, problems solved.

This King brings the energy of security and contentment arrived at through practicality. This card is often connected with property and/or keeping promises. With its emphasis on stability, it's a favorable card for employment and/or business.

Reversed: insecurity, greed, corruption.

This energy is not to be trusted; there is corruption afoot and dishonorable behavior is indicated, possibly due to an obsession with sensual delights and material goods. This could be in the form of someone who doesn't repay debts or is dishonest in dealings with property. At the very least, a miserly attitude is at work. Beware of the actions of others when money is their only motivation.

SECTION THREE

APPROACHING A TAROT READING

GETTING STARTED

It's important to recognize that the art of reading Tarot is, first and foremost, intuitive.

There are no strict rules, and while there is a lot of general consensus on card meanings, there are also differences among decks, reading styles, and so on. Often, it's not really the stated meaning behind a card that's going to inform you about your situation, but how the card and its imagery make you feel.

It can take years to fully master the art of Tarot reading, because of the fact that it is such an intuitive process. Just as if you were learning a musical instrument, you grow more confident with practice.

A PRACTICE EXERCISE FOR READING THE CARDS

The following exercise is good for practicing the art of noticing and "listening" to the cards. It can also be used on its own as a simple five minute tarot card reading.

Begin by identifying a question—something you can't know the answer to for certain, but want to know. If you're very new to Tarot, you might want to start with a very simple question.

Write the question down on a slip of paper, fold it up, and set it aside. Shuffle your deck for a moment, cards facing away from you, staying focused on your question. When you feel ready, select a card at random. Set the rest of the deck aside, and let go of the question.

(Note: If you don't have access to a deck yet, you can find images of cards online—try to use the first one you find. And if the Minor Arcana in your deck doesn't contain illustrations of people or scenes, be sure to choose a Major Arcana card. You could pull these from the deck and shuffle them separately.)

Turn the card over to reveal it, then quickly turn it back. What is the main thing you remember? What stood out as your very first impression?

For example, if you drew the 3 of Wands from the Waite-Smith deck, you might first notice the back of the figure in the center of the card, and possibly a vague sense that there are three long staffs surrounding the figure.

Now look at the card again. What else do you see?

This time, you might identify the figure as a man, and take in his right arm holding one of the staffs.

What do you *feel* as you continue to look at the card? Does the card seem to depict a peaceful feeling? A sorrowful one? Pay attention to any "gut feelings" that arise, no matter how subtle. This is your intuition, activated by the energy of the card.

Now, rather than trying to take in the whole picture, focus on noticing the smaller details.

You'll see that the figure is facing what looks to be a desert, with a mountain range in the background. A green swath of fabric hangs over the figure's left shoulder. What other colors are present? What other details do you see, however minute?

After you've spent time with each detail, "zoom out" and take another look at the picture as a whole. Imagine the image as a frozen scene in a larger story. Try to discern what the action is. What is happening? *Why* might it be happening? Is this man about to cross this wide open land? Or has he possibly just come from crossing it, and is looking back on how far he's come? Use the details as clues.

If you can, describe what you're seeing out loud, and/or jot down your impressions in a notebook.

What messages might this card be trying to communicate, based solely on what you see? Keep teasing it out, remembering that there are no right or wrong answers.

When you've given the card a thorough consideration, unfold the question you asked at the beginning of this exercise. Think about your observations in light of this question. Which of the details and/or possible messages seem significant? Feel free to explore this for as long as you would like. At some point, you should have some degree of a clear insight to your question.

If, after quite some time, you don't experience any kind of "answer," try again with a new card. And again, let go of any anxiety or self-consciousness about "getting it right." Tarot is an art, not a science.

READING FOR YOURSELF

It's probably ideal if your first experience with the Tarot involves someone else performing a reading for you, so you can get a sense of how the "unseen" can communicate clearly through this tool, without any interference of self-doubt about your ability to interpret the cards.

However, if this isn't possible, don't let it stop you—it's not an absolute requirement. Plenty of Tarot readers have only ever read their own cards, and find it very rewarding.

However, there *are* potential pitfalls here, as you may be unconsciously inclined to interpret your cards in a *favorable* light, stretching or even changing the meaning you normally associate with the card until it fits with what you want the answer to be. Be watchful for this tendency, as it's only human nature to be attached to certain outcomes, but it isn't doing you any good to ignore what the cards are telling you.

There are some people who avoid reading for themselves altogether, for the opposite reason—they're afraid that unwarranted negative messaging will come through, possibly because fear, rather than desire, will manipulate their interpretations.

This is something you'll need to decide for yourself, but if you can maintain a fair amount of objectivity, you can learn much about yourself and the Tarot as you practice reading on your own. You will also have a better handle on the cards, and therefore more confidence, as you read for others.

THE PROCESS OF A READING

Before beginning a reading, spend some time thinking about what you'd like to know from the cards. (If you're reading for someone else, it helps to have them state their question aloud, but it's not absolutely necessary.) The question should be open-ended—"yes or no" questions are generally unsuccessful, particularly for beginning readers. These questions will be the focal point of the reading.

You'll also need to decide what kind of spread you want to work with.

A spread is a set pattern for laying down the cards, with each card placed in a specific location and in a specific order. Each position in the pattern provides a particular angle on the situation you're asking about.

Generally speaking, each card has two possible sets of meanings, depending on whether they are placed upright or reversed. Perhaps more importantly, however, the cards in a layout interact with each other, so that their meanings are nuanced by the overall makeup of the spread. The layout is kind of like a story, with each individual card representing one aspect of the story. The reading is most effective when you read all of it together, because each card is connected and will affect the others.

As you or the querent shuffles the cards, keep your focus on the question. You can even repeat the question a few times, if it helps.

Continue to shuffle the cards until the querent feels that the time is right to stop. After shuffling, it's traditional to cut the deck, though not all readers do, at least not for every reading. The deck may be cut between one and three times, usually, and may be split into piles or put back together into one. When it comes to choosing the cards, you can take them off the top of the pile (or piles), or you can fan out the pile and choose each card from any point in it. Try a few different methods as you develop your own approach.

As for when to turn the cards over to reveal their images, this also varies among different traditions.

Some people like to flip them as soon as they take them from the deck, then lay them in their position in the spread. Others lay them face-down and wait to find out their identities until all the cards are drawn. At this point, they might turn all the cards at once, to get a general overview of what is on the table before they start reading each card individually. This can be particularly helpful for getting a better sense of how the cards are interacting with each other, before diving into the specifics. Others find it easier to turn over and contemplate one card at a time, like reading and absorbing one chapter of a story at a time before moving onto the next. Experimenting with both options can help you determine what works best for you.

It is important to remember that reading the Tarot is a task of intuition. While this guide provides general card interpretations along with two common types of readings, consulting the Tarot isn't as simple as reading a book. The meaning of each card in relation to the place it sits in the spread isn't always going to be straightforward or simple, and the difference between interpretations for upright and reversed isn't always clear cut, as each can be thought of as representing a different angle of the same theme.

If you think about it, rigidly sticking to one of two straightforward and clear meanings usually wouldn't provide much insight. Remember to think about the situation, the question, the person you're reading for, and the influences that the card's position in the spread might have.

There are probably hundreds of different spreads that you can use in Tarot readings. Each distinct layout will give you a different reading, and some are better suited than others for any given question.

Some people theorize that the more complicated the spread, the more difficult the required skill level will be, but this isn't necessarily true. It's true that the more cards you involve, the more factors you will need to consider, but the basic principle of reading the cards is going to be the same. It's just that there's more to the story.

Two of the most popular spreads are the Three-Card Spread and the Celtic Cross. The first is quite simple while the latter is somewhat complex, but each is helpful to those seeking to get acquainted with the Tarot.

INTRODUCING
TAROT SPREADS

THE THREE-CARD SPREAD

The number three has always had special significance in Wicca and Paganism, as well as many other religious and mystical traditions, perhaps because it is the number of points required to create a triangle, the first tangible form of reality.

The Three-Card Spread is an excellent first layout for a beginner. It's perfect for finding answers to relatively simple questions and makes for a good practice layout when getting acquainted with a new deck. It can be done fairly quickly, so you can seek answers on the fly when needed. And it's a good way to remind yourself that even the most seemingly complicated questions can often be answered relatively simply.

Another advantage of the Three-Card Spread is that there is more than one way to read it.

Each of the three cards represents a particular aspect of the situation involved in the question, but you can vary the meanings of the positions to tailor your reading around your particular issue. But the best place to start is probably with the most basic version of the spread: the Past, Present, and Future reading.

In this layout, the present is the card in the center, the past is the card on the left, and the future is on the right.

The cards are usually laid face-down, either from left to right, or, in some traditions, beginning in the center, then left, then right. Whether to begin in the center or on the left is a personal preference. Reading the present card first can reveal the angle of the situation the cards are speaking to, which might help you see the past in a new light. Conversely, starting with the past can help you confirm that the cards are answering the question you asked in a way that makes sense to you. Go with your instincts here, or try both approaches to see which seems to work best for you.

There are many, many variations on the simple Three-Card Spread. Below are a few more to try. Keep in mind that you can designate a different order than suggested here. In the first variation, for example, you might want the situation card in the center, rather than on the left. Just be sure to be clear about what stands for what in your own mind as you choose and lay down the cards. It can be helpful to identify the position as you lay the card down, so that, for example, as you lay down card #1 you say "The situation at hand" aloud.

For learning how to understand a situation

1. The situation at hand
2. Underlying factors affecting the situation
3. The resolution of the situation

For learning how to understand relationships

1. What you want to gain from a specific relationship
2. What the other person involved wants to gain from the relationship
3. The direction that the relationship is moving in

For advice on a difficult decision

1. One viable option
2. A second viable option
3. What you should know before you make a decision

For self-insight

1. How you see your identity
2. The path you're on at this moment
3. Your potential if you stay on this path

Remember that these are not the only possible configurations for the Three-Card Spread. As you gain experience with the Tarot, you can learn to design your own readings by changing the designations of each position according to the kind of answers you're seeking.

THE CELTRIC CROSS SPREAD

Of course, the Three-Card Spread can really only speak to three facets of a question. Often, we want a more complex look at a situation that goes beyond what three cards can tell us.

Perhaps the most commonly used layout in tarot readings is the Celtic Cross Spread. This spread typically involves ten cards, providing more opportunities to see different angles of a situation.

In a complex spread like this, it's important to remember that the cards are all connected. You won't get as much out of it if you attempt to simply read it piece by piece, as though each card were its own independent story. You might still get some useful information this way, but you'll miss out on deeper parts of your readings.

If this seems difficult at first, don't worry. With practice and time, you'll find it easier to see how the cards influence each other in your readings. Just be sure to get in the habit of looking at your layout as a whole, and you will begin to get a sharper sense of how the cards are interacting.

Once laid out, the cards in this spread resemble a cross (hence the name), accompanied by a four-card vertical line to the right. With so many cards used in one spread, it can be difficult to visualize how the cards are arranged, so here's a simple diagram of the Celtic Cross Spread.

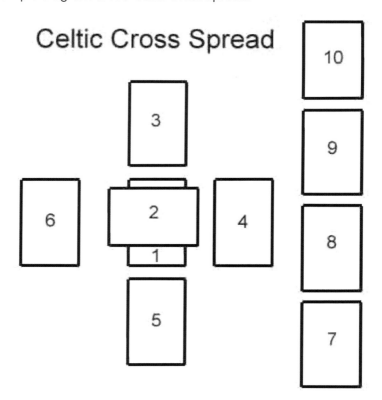

Celtic Cross Spread

If you want more explanation, the meaning and location of each position is as follows:

1. The first card is placed face up and perpendicular to your body. It represents the question that is being asked and can be considered the foundation of the reading. It also represents the present and the querent's state of mind regarding the question.

2. The second card is set down across the first one. It represents the obstacles and issues that need to be dealt with in the present. You may draw a card that seems to have a positive meaning for this position, but some kind of challenge is still being indicated, even if it's simply an overpowering desire for the outcome suggested by the card. Remember that the ways in which we focus on and go about trying to get what we want can be the very things preventing us from getting it!

3. The third card is placed just above the first two cards. It represents the querent's "higher self" or guiding influences as they apply to the situation. This could also represent the querent's goals, and what they want to get out of this situation. It may indicate what the querent has consciously been doing in their attempt to solve the issue at hand.

4. The fourth card is set down just beneath the first two. It represents the querent's subconscious and will reveal the personal struggles as well as positive influences from their past.

5. The fifth card is placed on the left side of the first two. It represents the past and events that are departing from the present focus. What is read in this card might tell you what happened that put the querent in this situation. It is often said that we are meant to learn from the past, so this card could be indicative of something that the querent can learn from in light of the current situation.

6. The sixth card is placed on the right side of the first two. It represents the events that will take place in the immediate future. This outcome could be directly linked to the decisions that the person being read has made in regards to the question at hand. This is by no means the end-all final outcome, but rather the next step on the journey.

7. The seventh card is placed to the right of the cross

created by the first six cards, in vertical alignment with cards 1-5, but with the bottom edge just below the bottom edge of card 4. This is often called the "advice card," providing an indication of what the querent should do (or stop doing) in order to address the situation, and may also reflect the influences and atmosphere immediately affecting the querent. We can always learn from our mistakes, so remember to think carefully about everything that's already been uncovered in the reading, and consider it in light of what's being revealed here.

8. The eighth card is placed right above the seventh card. It represents how other people see the situation and the question at hand. It also represents the people, events, and energies that will influence the outcome of the querent's situation. It will indicate the outside factors that are out of their control.

9. The ninth card is placed right above the eighth card. It represents the querent's hopes, dreams, and fears about the future. This can be the most difficult card in the spread to read, as it is tapping into the feelings of the querent. So if you're reading for someone else, you have to have an intrinsic understanding of the other cards in the layout, what they mean to the querent, and the querent in general, all in regard to the question being asked. People keep their fears guarded, so it may not be obvious. Remember that hopes and fears are connected and intertwined. (For instance, someone who has a desire to get on stage and perform may also happen to have stage fright.) If this particular card is too difficult to decipher on its own, you can always draw a second card and read them together to get a clearer meaning.

10. The tenth card is placed right above the ninth card. It represents the long-term outcome of the situation based on the other cards in the reading, and it may be interpreted by the querent as the answer to the question that prompted the reading. However, this card is only an assumption based on the way that the querent is currently handling the situation. It's possible that the querent will not enjoy this part of the reading, if the interpretation is not favorable. If that is the case, it's extra beneficial to review the previous cards and discuss the reading as a whole, to help advise them on how to proceed. Remind them that it is up to them to make whatever changes that they deem necessary in order to avoid an undesirable outcome.

TAKING THE NEXT STEPS

If you want to explore the Tarot for yourself, it's ideal to have your own deck, some time to set aside, and a good space for practicing this fascinating form of divination.

If you have friends who read Tarot or are interested in learning with you, this can broaden your experience and make it even more fun. Either way, below you'll find useful tips for getting started on your path.

CHOOSING A TAROT DECK

These days, the variety of published Tarot decks available for purchase is unprecedented.

There are "traditional" decks like the *Waite-Smith*, with detailed scenes that are central to the interpretation of the cards, or the *Tarot of Marseille,* where the illustrations for the Minor Arcana are abstract. Many of the contemporary decks are based on one of these two.

Then there are many "non-traditional" decks that use completely different characters and archetypes for the Major Arcana, as well as different names for the suits.

Some publishers have created "novelty" decks that commemorate specific themes, occult traditions, and even aspects of popular culture—I'm told there's even a *Simpson's* tarot deck!

Each departure from the more standard decks provides an opportunity to expand into new realms of meaning within the overall world of the Tarot. If you're just starting out, however, it probably makes more sense to stick with something in the more traditional category, and branch out to more unusual decks once you get more experience.

Each deck has its own personality, mood, and style, and it's likely that no two decks will provide quite the same quality of reading experience. Furthermore, every reader is unique, so a deck that your friend swears by might simply not work for you. Some people feel more inspired by intricate designs, while others prefer less visual information. The way you feel about the look of your deck is likely to affect the quality of your readings, so be sure to choose something you'll enjoy.

Tarot cards can be bought online, but it's ideal to go to a store in person to choose your deck—many bookstores will have a reasonably wide selection. There, you can look at the decks closely and, more importantly, hold them in your hands.

Get a real feel for each deck that catches your eye, and pick the one that you feel you relate to most strongly. If this is your first deck, then you might want to pick a deck that comes with an instruction booklet. These booklets generally contain very brief card meanings, as well as a model spread or two, and can help you get acquainted with the deck more quickly.

If your deck does come with a booklet, you may find that there are similarities and differences when compared to the card meanings provided in this guide. Similarities can offer you more shades of understanding to add to those associated with your deck. In the case of differences, you may find that the more logical interpretation comes from your deck's instructions, but at times, this may not be the case.

The main drawback of most booklets is that it's hard to determine an interpretation from the two or three words per card that they provide, so don't rely too heavily on them! Always go with your intuition first.

If Tarot cards are not available anywhere in your area, then be sure to spend some time researching your online choices. Look closely at the art featured for each deck and make note of any instinctive responses a particular picture or set of pictures creates in you. Remember, reading the Tarot is an intuitive art, right from the get-go. Don't commit to buying a deck if you don't feel completely sure about it!

After you've learned the basics of Tarot and worked with your first deck for some time, you'll find that reading the cards starts to come more easily to you. This might be the ideal time to challenge yourself by looking into other decks. You never know how inspirational a new deck might be, and reading new decks will help you grow in your understanding of Tarot reading as a whole.

GETTING ACQUAINTED WITH YOUR NEW DECK

The Tarot is like a complex, interesting new friend. It will take a while to get to know your cards, and there will be more and more information revealed as you deepen your relationship.

For your first encounter, you might want to fan the cards out in front of you, or briefly flip through so you get at least a glimpse of each card. Then, take some time to look at each card individually, giving it your full attention. Study the imagery, making an effort to notice the small details.

After you've "introduced yourself" to each card in the deck, do another round, this time familiarizing yourself with each card's assigned meanings as you study it. You'll want to do this more than once, obviously. You can't get to know everything about your new friend all in one sitting! If you can set aside time once a day, you'll learn faster and become more comfortable with your deck.

Some people will actually place their cards underneath their pillow at night, to aid the subconscious in absorbing the meanings of the cards while they sleep. You could try this with the whole deck, or try putting just one card at a time under the pillow, which can be useful for those cards that just seem harder to "get" than others.

Another way people form a connection or bond with their new cards is to charge them with their own personal energy. You can do this by laying them in the light of a full or new moon, meditating or praying over them, or moving them through the smoke of burning incense. Some people believe that their cards will have more power if they are kept inside of a special pouch or box, and/or stored with a specific type of crystal. This is, of course, up to you, but it's recommended that you maintain respectful care of the cards both when using them and storing them.

Taking the topic of personal energy further, some people believe that it is harmful to allow other people to touch their deck, as this may "contaminate" their cards with another person's negative fears, beliefs, and anxieties. Your cards are personal, and they are your portal to wisdom of the Universe, so this theory is worth thinking about. If there are people in your life who seem to have "toxic energy," you might want to keep your cards away from them. However, know that you can also always "reset" the energy of your cards by shuffling them for long enough to realign them with your energy. You will know instinctively when you've achieved this.

When reading for others, some people will do the shuffling for the querent, adhering to the notion that the energy of the cards should never be altered by someone else's hands. The only problem here is a conflicting belief that readings are more accurate when the querent does the shuffling. Use your best judgment here, but if you do have others handle your cards, be sure to "reset" them again before doing another reading.

CREATING A SACRED SPACE

An effective, useful Tarot reading requires more than just a deck of cards. The right environment is also important.

There's an energetic quality to a good Tarot reading, where information from the unseen dimensions becomes more readily available to the reader, and likely to the querent as well. This energy is far more enhanced in a calm, quiet, private space.

If you think about it, you're not likely to get good results in a noisy room with people coming and going, or with the television on in the background. You need to be able to focus your undivided attention on listening to what the cards have to say. It's very difficult to get a useful reading when you're trying to battle distractions! The more conducive your space is to divination, the more deep and insightful the reading is likely to be.

So how do you create a tranquil reading space? There are a few elements to consider, which can be identified as physical, mental, emotional, and spiritual. Each element has an impact on the quality of the reading and your overall experience with the Tarot.

The physical space includes everything in the tangible environment, whether you're at home in your room, out in public in a park or café, or in a beautiful, secluded natural setting. (If you can manage that third option, it can really be ideal!) First, you'll need a surface for laying out the cards, whether it be a table or a picnic blanket, as well as somewhere comfortable to sit. You'll also need at least some degree of privacy, meaning that if there are other people around, they won't be interrupting or observing you in an intrusive way. If you're indoors, try to keep clutter in the area to a minimum. Being distracted by anything in your physical environment can "break the spell" of the intuitive link between the cards, yourself, and the information coming in from out there in the Universe. So be sure to take these factors into consideration before beginning a reading.

The mental space is, of course, inside your head, but is just as real and important as anything you can physically see. Thoughts, hopes, anxieties, and stressors take up space in your mind. If you are plagued with too many other thoughts, the cards you draw may not add up to anything that makes sense to you.

You can work on making sure that you're calm and centered by creating your own pre-reading ritual. For example, if you have candles around the room, you can begin by lighting each one, taking your time and focusing on the flame as you go. You can work through meditative breathing exercises, and let yourself tune into the room, leaving out the rest of the world. Meditation music or recorded nature sounds can be helpful in this regard as well. Of course, sometimes mundane thoughts are too stubborn to go away. If you find that for whatever reason, you just can't clear your mind, try writing down whatever thoughts are persisting and then set the paper aside. Think of it as though you're putting those distracting thoughts into their own little lock box, tucked away for later.

If you're reading for someone else, it's a good idea to advise them to take a deep breath before concentrating on their question and shuffling the cards. You can use the "lock box" technique with them, too, if it becomes clear that there are extraneous thoughts that won't go away. The state of mind of the querent is possibly the most important element of a quality reading—even if the cards speak to some other aspect of their life beyond the question they've come to ask.

Emotional space and mental space are generally intertwined, but where thoughts tend to come and go rather easily, emotions can be harder to release. It's one thing to be preoccupied by your to-do list for the next day, and quite another to be worried about the health of someone you love.

If you find yourself in any kind of emotional distress, it might be not be the best time to do a reading. Then again, if you're reading for yourself, the cards may be able to offer you advice on working through the emotion, or, if it's related to a problem you're having, addressing the source of it directly. You and/or the querent can also take a few deep breaths to release any unwanted emotional energy. As you breathe in, visualize yourself being filled with healing love and light. As you exhale, visualize any pain, fear, stress, or other unwanted feelings leaving your body and drifting out into the Universe.

Many Tarot readers would argue that there is no separation between physical space and the spiritual realm—just a division between the seen and unseen. Whatever your take on the meaning of the word "spiritual," it is important to acknowledge and respect the flow of energy that connects you to the Universe and informs your intuition during the reading. Tapping into this "space" in an instantaneous way can be challenging, which is why it's recommended that you clear mental and emotional "debris" before sitting down to read the cards.

You can also make use of candles, crystals, mandalas, or any other objects that help you connect with the unseen energies around you. Meditation is useful in this regard as well, along with simply verbally asking the Universe for the calm and clarity you'll need to interpret what the cards are telling you. You can try saying something simple but meaningful, like, "I open myself up to becoming an instrument of the truth and I will use this insight to honor the divine spirit that dwells within all of us." Meditation after a Tarot reading is also useful, to gently return yourself to "ordinary" space. This is particularly recommended if you find yourself feeling drained or out of sorts after a reading, which is not uncommon, particularly when reading for others.

CONCLUSION

Now that you've gained a basic overview of the Tarot and its possibilities, you can chart a path of your own by reading more, practicing, and enjoying spending time with the cards.

Remember to trust your intuition along the way. Don't approach a reading the way you'd approach a book report in school. There are designated meanings to each card and instructions for interpreting them, but it's not meant to be the kind of thing that you need a book to guide you through forever. Pay attention to the ideas that pop into your mind, and to the way that you feel when interacting with the cards. Don't doubt your instincts just because instructions in a book contradict what you see in the cards.

It's not always going to be easy in the beginning, but once you get more comfortable with your deck and become better versed in the art, you'll have more and more moments when the cards are clearly speaking to you directly.

It's a good idea to take notes on your readings before putting the cards away. You can go back to them later to see which of your interpretations panned out, and deepen your understanding of the cards through your own experience of life.

While you're first starting out, you might want to make goals for yourself and/or designate a specific amount of time every day to improving your skills. Don't become discouraged if you don't get it right away. It takes time to become a fluid reader of the Tarot, but it's an incredibly fulfilling journey!

I will leave you with that thought, as it is now time for you to start your own journey, and begin listening to and interpreting the cards for yourself. For those of you who want to know more, I have included several suggested sources for further reading, as other author's work and interpretations can help you get a deeper understanding to the subject of Tarot.

I sincerely hoped you enjoyed learning about Tarot with me, and I hope you find Tarot as rewarding as I do!

Thank you one more time for reading.

SUGGESTIONS FOR FURTHER READING

There are numerous books about the Tarot. Many are devoted to a particular deck, such as the Waite-Smith or the Tarot of Marseilles. The following books are useful for beginners and those with some level of experience. This list is by no means definitive, but rather a good place to start.

Barbara Moore, *Tarot for Beginners: A Practical Guide to Reading the Cards* (2010)

Sandor Konraad, *Classic Tarot Spreads* (1985)

Sallie Nichols, *Jung and Tarot: An Archetypal Journey* (1980)

Rachel Pollack, *Seventy-Eight Degrees of Wisdom: A Book of Tarot* (2007)

Robert Place, *The Tarot: History, Symbolism, and Divination* (2005)

Mary K. Greer, *Who Are You in the Tarot?: Discover your Birth and Year Cards and Uncover Your Destiny* (2011)

Alejandro Jodorowsky and Marianne Costa, *The Way of Tarot: The Spiritual Teacher in the Cards* (2009)

DID YOU ENJOY *TAROT FOR BEGINNERS?*

Again let me thank you for purchasing and reading this guide.

There are a number of great books on the topic, so I really appreciate you choosing this one.

If you enjoyed the book, I'd like to ask for a small favor in return. If possible, I'd love for you to take a couple of minutes to leave a review for this book on Amazon.

Your feedback will help me to make improvements to this guide, as well as writing books on other topics that might be of interest to you. Hopefully this will allow me to create even better guides in future!

OTHER BOOKS BY LISA CHAMBERLAIN

FREE GIFT REMINDER

Here's one final reminder of the free downloadable book I'm offering, as I'd hate for you to miss out!

Wicca: Book of Wiccan Spells is ideal for any Wiccans looking to start practicing Witchcraft. It includes a collection of ten spells that I have deemed suitable for beginners.

You can download it by visiting:

www.wiccaliving.com/bonus

I hope you enjoy it!

Printed in Great Britain
by Amazon